FLYTE

faith. life. together.

VOLUME 1

2011 LifeWay
016 Reprint

o part of this work may be reproduced or transmitted in any form or by any means, ectronic or mechanical, including photocopying and recording, or by any information orage or retrieval system, except as may be expressly permitted in writing by the ublisher. Requests for permission should be addressed in writing to LifeWay, One feWay Plaza, Nashville, TN 37234-0172.

BN 978-1-4158-7060-0
em 005399874

ewey Decimal Classification Number: 220.07
ubject Heading: BIBLE—STUDY AND TEACHING/PRETEENS
rinted in the United States of America

ds Ministry Publishing
feWay Church Resources
ne LifeWay Plaza
ashville, Tennessee 37234-0172

e believe that the Bible has God for its author; salvation for its end; and truth, without ny mixture of error, for its matter and that all Scripture is totally true and trustworthy. To view LifeWay's doctrinal guideline, please visit *www.lifeway.com/doctrinalguideline*.

l Scripture quotations are taken from the Holman Christian Standard Bible®, copyright 299, 2000, 2002, 2003, 2009 by Holman Bible Publishers. Used by permission.

CONTENTS

UNIT 1: HEAVEN

- What Is Heaven?
- How Do I Go to Heaven? 1
- Do I Have to Be Baptized to Go to Heaven? 2
- How Can I Help My Friends Go to Heaven? 2

Unit 2: CHANGE 3

- Why Is My Body Changing? 3
- How Is My Body Changing? 4
- How Can I Cope with My Changing Body? 4
- Why Do I Care What People Think of Me? 5

Unit 3: FAMILY 5

- What Is a Perfect Family? 6
- Is My Family Broken? 6
- Is There Hope for My Family? 7
- How Can My Family Work Together? 7

Bonus: Living High or Higher Living? 8

FLYTE PLAN

FLYTE: faith. life. together. is designed to be the most relevant and easy-to-use preteen curriculum available. FLYTE answers preteens' toughest questions by actively engaging them in the study of God's Word.

Get Started

- During this portion of the Bible study, preteens will get excited about the session's subject.
- Each Get Started section has a countdown timer to help preteens know when the session will begin. Cue the video to the "Takeoff" portion of the DVD and play the episode three minutes prior to your designated start time.
- A "Weird of the Day" will appear immediately after the countdown clock reaches zero. The "Weird of the Day" may or may not (most of the time NOT!) have anything to do with the session topic.
- Preteens will then complete a high-energy activity to really get them excited about the topic and to get them thinking about what they will be learning.
- Following the high-energy activity, preteens will be challenged with a more thoughtful activity to gauge their current knowledge of the session topic.
- A funny video will regularly be used to help preteens further engage in the session topic. Videos are used in different sections of each session in order to keep the preteens' attention.

Faith: God's Answer

- Each Faith section involves preteens actively engaging in God's Word to seek out Scripture about the session topic.
- Preteens will study a unit memory passage during each four-week unit. Be sure to show preteens the music video several times during each unit, as it will reinforce the memory passage. Music videos can be found under the title "Music Video" on each session's video menu.
- Preteens will learn the background of the Scripture reference, as well as tips for applying the Scripture to their lives.
- Occasional optional Bible study videos are available on the session's video menu to reinforce the Bible study.
- Videos will regularly be used to help preteens understand the topic from a biblical perspective.

Life: World's Answer

- During this portion of the Bible study, preteens will be encouraged to discuss and explore the world's opinion about the session topic.
- The Life section will confront the untruths preteens learn through the media, television, their friends, and sometimes their family members.
- Preteens will learn that although not everything the world tells them is bad, there is only one perfect truth—and that comes from God. Preteens can know God's truth through studying the Bible, seeking godly friends and leaders, and fellowshipping with other believers.
- Videos will regularly be used to help preteens understand the world's point of view.

Together: My Answer

- During this portion of the Bible study, preteens will create their response to the question of the day.
- Preteens are encouraged to look at God's answer that they learned during the Faith section and formulate a response to the session's topic with the awareness of how the world views the topic.
- This is the point in FLYTE at which preteens are encouraged to develop their own biblical worldview so that they are prepared to answer with God's truth when the world asks them questions.
- Videos will regularly be used to help preteens further develop their responses to the session topic.
- Over and Out reiterates in clear, simple terms the main points of the session.

UNIT 1
HEAVEN

Memory Passage: Isaiah 57:15

Session 1: What Is Heaven?
- Bible passage: Revelation 21:1–22:5
- Heaven is neither boring nor simple. This week's session will help preteens get excited about an eternity in heaven.

Session 2: How Do I Go to Heaven?
- Bible passage: Acts 16:25-31
- There is only one path into heaven. This session will teach preteens how they can follow the path to heaven.

Session 3: Do I Have to Be Baptized to Go to Heaven?
- Bible passage: Matthew 3:13-17; Luke 23:32-49
- Baptism is not required for entrance into heaven. This session will explore baptism as an act of obedience to God.

Session 4: How Can I Help My Friends Go to Heaven?
- Bible passage: Ephesians 1:7; John 3:16; Matthew 7:21; James 2:13; Romans 3:23; Luke 13:3; Romans 10:9; John 10:10; 14:3
- True friends cannot risk allowing their friends to go to hell. Christians should be links in the chain to help friends go to heaven.

Mark Browning wrote the Heaven study. He teaches preteen Bible study at First Baptist Church of Oak Grove, Missouri. Mark also teaches writing and literature at Johnson County Community College.

UNIT 1 FLYTE PREP

Other FLYTE Necessities:

FLYTE DVD
The FLYTE DVD has everything you need to enhance media usage with your preteens. Take advantage of the great DVD episodes every week: a countdown clock, Weird of the Day video, teaching video, memory passage music video, and much more.

FLYTE CD-ROM
All the teacher helps, articles, and activity helps you could ever want are found on the CD-ROM. And, because it's important to keep parents in the loop, we've included parent letters for you to e-mail or mail parents (like with a stamp!) to give them a heads-up as to what you will be studying. Take time to explore the entire FLYTE CD-ROM so you don't miss something awesome.

FLYTE Learner Magazine
The FLYTE magazine for preteens is designed to really get your preteens' attention. Exciting graphics, relevant articles, and fun activities will enhance your session as well as provide a resource that preteens can take home and use for future reference. You'll want to buy one for every preteen in your class!

For updates and information, find FLYTE online at
www.lifeway.com/flyte

Session 1: What Is Heaven?
You will need:
- DVD: What Is Heaven? Episodes
- CD-ROM Item 1
- FLYTE magazine (pages 7-9)
- disposable cups
- index cards
- 4 large sheets of craft paper
- washable markers
- stopwatch

Session 2: How Do I Go to Heaven?
You will need:
- DVD: How Do I Go to Heaven? Episodes
- CD-ROM Items 1, 2, 3, 4
- FLYTE magazine (pages 10, 11)
- craft paper
- strips of paper
- copy paper
- masking tape
- sticky notes
- scissors

Session 3: Do I Have to Be Baptized to Go to Heaven?
You will need:
- DVD: Do I Have to Be Baptized to Go to Heaven? Episodes
- CD-ROM Items 1, 5
- FLYTE magazine (pages 13-15)
- 9 equally-sized photographs

Session 4: How Can I Help My Friends Go to Heaven?
You will need:
- DVD: How Can I Help My Friends Go to Heaven? Episodes
- CD-ROM Items 6, 7
- FLYTE magazine (pages 16-18)
- 150 paperclips or more
- watch or timer
- whiteboard
- dry erase markers

WHAT IS HEAVEN?

Session Overview

memory activity, an inventory of heaven, a look at different views f heaven, and a study of the real heaven as described in the Book of evelation will help preteens value heaven as the place for spending ternity with Jesus.

Teacher Bible Study >>>

sk five people to describe heaven, and you'll probably hear ve different answers. In fact, ask five people in your church. The sponses will probably still be quite different. In Mark 10:35-37, ames and John asked to sit at the right hand and left hand of Jesus in is glory. Throughout the account of the Last Supper in John's Gospel, e apostles did not quite understand where Jesus was going.

Take a look at John 14:1-4. In this well-known passage, Jesus talked f preparing a place for His followers. In the King James Version, Jesus oke of "many mansions." When you envision this passage, do you e Jesus preparing a place with a tool belt and lumber? Do those mansions" resemble the most opulent houses you have ever seen?

The reality of heaven transcends both the human imagination and e human language. When Isaiah visited heaven in Isaiah 6, the ible says that God's robe (or the train of His robe) filled the heavenly mple. Can you imagine that? Yet there are still other things in the mple. Read the description of the seraphim. Can you imagine them ithout reference to earthly creatures?

When you meet with preteens for this session, you will not have a erfect understanding of heaven. By the time you achieve that, you ill no longer be teaching; however, you can still learn a lot about eaven's reality from the details God has provided in His Word.

ray. Ask God to give you as clear a view of heaven as you can chieve. Ask Him to help the preteens you teach understand not only e reality of heaven but its importance to eternal life.

FLYTE Plan

Heaven is neither boring nor simple. This week's session will help preteens get excited about an eternity in heaven.

Bible Study
Revelation 21:1–22:5

Memory Passage
Isaiah 57:15

Level of Biblical Learning
(Salvation): The Bible tells me God sent Jesus so I can have a personal relationship with God.

Get Ready
- "Heaven Session 1: Takeoff" (DVD)
- FLYTE magazine (page 7)
- disposable cups—Number the cups 1-10.
- index cards—Number the cards 1-10.
- stopwatch

Get Started >>>

Takeoff
- Play "Heaven Session 1: Takeoff" (DVD) three minutes before the designated start time for the session.
- Allow preteens a minute or two to talk about the Weird of the Day.

Number Rush
- Place the numbered cups at one side of the room.
- Display the numbered index cards in random order at the other side of the room.
- Instruct a volunteer to memorize the sequence of numbers from the cards and then run across the room to arrange the cups in the order of the cards.
- The player may run back to consult the cards if needed.
- Time each player. Add a 15-second penalty for each number the player has placed out of order.
- Allow each preteen to have a turn.
- OPTION: For groups of six or more, create enough cup sets for teams of three. Then allow teams to compete against each other.

Number Crunch
- Pick up a card set used in the previous activity and arrange the cards in random order.
- Challenge a volunteer to arrange the cups in the proper order without looking at your cards.
- After allowing a couple of volunteers to try, ask: "How difficult would it be to guess the order of the 10 numbers?"
- Explain that the odds of getting the numbers right are 3,628,800 to 1. In other words, there are approximately 3.6 million combinations of numbers they could arrange.
- Point out that guessing exactly what heaven is like would be even more difficult, but thankfully God gave some descriptions in the Bible.

Hollywood Heavens
- Distribute FLYTE magazines and direct preteens to "Hollywood Heavens" on page 7.
- Ask volunteers to think of movies in which heaven is depicted and write the titles on the lines.
- Guide preteens to discuss what each film seems to have gotten right or wrong about heaven.
- Conclude this activity by pointing out that people's opinions of heaven aren't very important. What matters is the truth about heaven, which preteens can begin to understand by consulting God's Word.

Faith: God's Answer >>>

Memory Passage: Isaiah 57:15

- Ask preteens to read the memory passage from the "Isaiah 57:15 Poster" (Item 1) in the following manner: Preteens to your left should read the first two lines of the verse, followed by those on your right. Repeat, reversing the roles of the groups.
- Encourage preteens to memorize the verse over the course of the unit.
- Challenge preteens to open their Bibles to Isaiah 57:15 and answer the following questions:
  » Who is the writer of the verse? (*Isaiah*)
  » What do you learn about Isaiah from the first few lines? (*God speaks to him.*)
  » Where does God live? And with whom? (*In a high and holy place with the oppressed and lowly of spirit*)
- Allow preteens to discuss what they think this verse means.
- OPTION: Show "Revive" (DVD).

Study the Bible: Revelation 21:1-22:5

- Guide preteens to locate Revelation 21 in their Bibles.
- Point out that the Book of Revelation was written by the apostle John, who saw heaven in a vision.
- Allow a volunteer to read Revelation 21:1-8 aloud.
- Ask preteens to answer the following questions:
  » Is the heaven and earth described in these verses the same one existing today? (*No.*)
  » What people will go to this new heaven? (*God's children, those who are victorious.*)
  » Who will live with these people? (*God*)

Heavenly Inventory

- Call attention to the large sheet of paper attached to the focal wall.
- Ask preteens to call out what they imagine heaven will look like. Record their answers on the sheet of paper.
- Offer suggestions if preteens are having a hard time thinking of descriptions. (Examples: streets of gold, pearly gates, and angels.)
- Remind them that the descriptions don't have to be accurate; you are just compiling a list of all the different opinions about what heaven might be like.

The True Inventory

- Form three groups. Instruct the first group to consider Revelation 21:9-18. Assign the second group Revelation 21:19-27. The final group will cover Revelation 22:1-5.
- Distribute markers and a large sheet of paper to each group. Ask the groups to carefully read their assigned passages, writing down any descriptions of what heaven will be like.

Get Ready
- "John's Vision of Heaven (FLYTE Option)," "Revive (Music Video)" (DVD)
- Item 1: "Isaiah 57:15 Poster" (CD-ROM)
- FLYTE magazine (page 7)
- 4 large sheets of craft paper—Attach one sheet to a focal wall.
- washable markers

UNIT 1 HEAVEN

- Encourage them to list the Scripture reference for each description.
- Guide each group to post its list on the wall near the list made during "Heavenly Inventory."
- Direct preteens to "The True Inventory" on page 7 of their magazines. Ask preteens to refer to the posters the groups created and list in their magazines items that will be found in heaven.

Beyond Comparison

- Guide preteens to compare the lists the groups created to the list that was created during "Heavenly Inventory."
- Cross off any descriptions on the "Heavenly Inventory" list that do not appear on the lists created by the groups.
- Allow preteens to vote on their favorite description, the description that sounds most fun, and the description that is most confusing.
- Remind preteens that the list is not all-inclusive; there are some things that are still unknown about heaven.

Option: John's Vision of Heaven

- Play "John's Vision of Heaven" (DVD) if time allows.
- Allow for a brief discussion of the host's view of the passage.

Life: World's Answer >>>

ameshow: Views of Heaven

- Cue the DVD to "Lameshow: Views of Heaven" and guide preteens to open their FLYTE magazines to "Views of Heaven" on page 8.
- Introduce the video by asking preteens how they believe people might answer the question, "What is heaven like?"
- Explain that some of the views of heaven in the video are pretty odd or incorrect.
- Play the DVD.
- Guide preteens to write down the incorrect views of heaven they saw in the video.

My Type of Heaven

- Direct the group's attention to the article "My Type of Heaven" on pages 8 and 9.
- Allow preteens to determine which of the incorrect ideas from the "Views of Heaven" video belong in each type of heaven as described in the magazine article. For instance: Would any of the views presented belong in the Amusement Park Heaven?

he Center of Heaven

- Point out the vast differences between the different types of heaven described in the magazine.
- Allow preteens to share any aspects of these false heavens that they find appealing.
- Lead a discussion about how each view of heaven in the article falls short of the Bible's descriptions.
- Point out that one thing missing from each of these heaven views is God's presence.
- Ask a volunteer to re-read Revelation 22:1-5.
- Emphasize that God has always been and always will be at the center of heaven.

Get Ready
- "Lameshow: Views of Heaven (Feature)" (DVD)
- FLYTE magazine (pages 8, 9)

Together: My Answer >>>

Looking Back on Looking Forward

• Direct preteens to locate the "Looking Back on Looking Forward" activity in the magazine (page 9).
• Ask each preteen to consider an event that he or she looked forward to with great anticipation: a vacation, a birthday, a new home, a holiday, and so forth.
• Direct preteens to complete the questions in the "Earthly Event" section of the activity. Allow volunteers to share their answers.
• Point out that these activities almost always let people down in some way. Vacations don't always go as planned, and birthdays are not always as exciting as you might have hoped.
• Allow preteens to complete the "Heavenly Event" section.
• Encourage them to compare and contrast their answers.
• Emphasize that heaven is something preteens can look forward to without risk of disappointment and without worrying that it will cease to amaze and delight. It will definitely be better than anyone could ever imagine.

Over and Out

• Dismiss preteens with these final thoughts:
  » Heaven is the destination for Christians.
  » Heaven is not about people's wishes and desires.
  » God is at the center of heaven.
• Pray. Thank God for providing a perfect and permanent home in heaven for Christians. Ask Him to help preteens better understand the promise and truth of their final destination.

HOW DO I GO TO HEAVEN?

Session Overview

...n escape game, active Bible study, survey of the world's opinion on ...etting to heaven, and a closer look at the Bible passage will help ...reteens recognize that there is only one way to get to heaven.

Teacher Bible Study >>>

...n its surface, today's Bible passage seems to have little to do with ...eaven. Read Acts 16:25-31. Paul told the jailer what he must do to be ...ved, but he did not specifically mention heaven in these verses. This ...ory seems to be more about getting out of jail than about getting ...to heaven. If you look closely, though, you can see a subtle but very ...mportant lesson being taught.

At the beginning of this passage, Paul and Silas were sitting in jail as ...isoners. The jailer sat outside of the bars, a free man. However, the ...les were actually reversed. It was Paul and Silas who sat carefree in ...ains, singing hymns to God. The jailer, as revealed in the aftermath ...f the earthquake, lived in fear. As soon as he believed his prisoners ...ad escaped, he drew his sword, ready to end his life.

The message of salvation, as explained by Paul in verse 31, seems ...be such a simple thing, yet it liberates. Paul and Silas had no fear ...they sat in the jail. They knew that, earthquake or not, freedom ...bondage, they had secured their entrance into heaven. The jailer, ...espite his apparent freedom, lived a prisoner's life. During this ...ssion, preteens will explore the question, "How do I go to heaven?" ...he answer is the simplest yet most profound of facts: "Believe on the ...rd Jesus and you will be saved."

...ay. Ask God to allow each preteen you teach to see his or her need ...ask the jailer's question. Pray that God will guide your actions and ...rds to help bring some or all of your class to Himself in heaven.

FLYTE Plan

There is only one path into heaven. This session will teach preteens how they can follow the path to heaven.

Bible Study
Acts 16:25-31

Memory Passage
Isaiah 57:15

Level of Biblical Learning
(Salvation): Without a Savior, the punishment for sin is eternal death and hell.

Get Ready
- "Heaven Session 2: Takeoff," "Knocking on Heaven's Door (Feature)" (DVD)
- craft paper—Cut into strips about 6 inches wide and 40 inches long. (Be mindful of larger preteens. You may need to cut longer strips to avoid embarrassment.)
- masking tape

Get Started >>>

Takeoff
- Play "Heaven Session 2: Takeoff" (DVD) three minutes before the designated start time for the session.
- Allow preteens a minute or two to talk about the Weird of the Day.

Breaking Free
- Group preteens into pairs, boys with boys and girls with girls. Give each pair a supply of paper strips and tape.
- Explain that today the challenge is for each participant to demonstrate an ability to escape.
- Instruct one preteen in each pair to stand with his arms straight at his side.
- Direct the other member of the pair to wrap a strip of paper around his partner, taping the strip securely. (If your paper is not very strong, begin with two layers.)
- Allow the bound preteens to break loose from the paper.
- Reverse the roles and repeat this process.
- Repeat this entire process again, this time using two strips of paper, one on top of the other, for each preteen.
- Continue the activity, increasing layers of paper until preteens are unable to escape.
- Identify and congratulate the preteen able to escape from the greatest number of layers.
- Share that some people believe that it is really hard to get into heaven, but preteens can know that God has made the way clear and attainable. Explain that they will learn more in today's session about how to get to heaven.

Door to Heaven
- Ask preteens to recall some of the information they learned last week about heaven.
- After discussing their answers, ask preteens if they remember anything about heaven having a door.
- Cue the DVD to "Knocking on Heaven's Door."
- Explain that the video they will watch was created a long time ago to explain how to get to heaven. Play the video.
- Ask the group to recall ways people in the video thought they could get to heaven. Did it perhaps seem too obvious or easy?
- Explain that today's session will explore the very simple and only way a person can ensure his or her entry into heaven.

Faith: God's Answer >>>

Memory Passage: Isaiah 57:15

- Place the "Isaiah 57:15 Poster" (Item 1) on a table.
- Lead preteens in reciting the verse twice together.
- Cover five of the words with sticky notes.
- Challenge preteens to recite the verse, supplying the covered words.
- As they begin to memorize the verse, cover more and different words. Finally, cover the entire poster and allow volunteers to recite the verse from memory.
- OPTION: Show "Revive" (DVD).

Isaiah Facts

- Distribute a pencil and one sticky note to each preteen.
- Tell preteens that you will read a list of facts about Isaiah, and they should write them on their sticky notes in order.
- Read the following list as fast as possible. Do not pause after each sentence.
  - » Isaiah means "Yahweh Saves."
  - » Isaiah was a prophet to the Southern Kingdom of Judah.
  - » His book is the first book of the Major Prophets in the Old Testament.
  - » The Book of Isaiah includes prophecy about the Messiah.
  - » Jesus read from the Book of Isaiah and then announced that He was the One to whom those Scriptures referred.[1]
- Poll preteens to see how many facts they were able to write down.
- Congratulate the preteen who was able to write down the most facts. Review the facts at a slower pace.
- Encourage preteens to mark the Book of Isaiah in their Bibles with their sticky notes.

Study the Bible: Acts 16:25-31

- Direct preteens to open their Bibles to Acts 16:25-31 and sit in chairs arranged in a circle. Explain that they will be playing the role of prisoners.
- Assign one or two players to serve as guards for the "prisoners." Instruct the guards to listen carefully to the Bible passage. Direct them to make an up-and-down motion with their hands whenever they hear a word ending in "-ing" and a circling motion when they hear a word ending in "-ed." Warn the guards that failure to give the proper signal will cause them to be placed in the prison.
- Instruct the prisoners to quickly stand up and sit down when they see the up-and-down motion. They should move one seat to the left when they see the circling motion. Point out that the prisoners should not move unless they see the guards' motions.
- Read the passage. Use the "Acts 16:25-31 Story" (Item 2), which has all of the action words marked. Do not pause or emphasize the action words. Do pause briefly when the prisoners are in

Get Ready

- "Revive (Music Video)" (DVD)
- Items 1, 2, 3, 4: "Isaiah 57:15 Poster," "Acts 16:25-31 Story," "ABC/FAITH Salvation Message," "Sharing Your Faith" (CD-ROM)
- FLYTE magazine (page 10)
- sticky notes

UNIT 1 HEAVEN

[1]Facts from *Holman Illustrated Bible Dictionary for Kids* (Nashville: B&H Publishing Group, 2010)

motion.

- If a guard fails to give the proper signal upon use of one of the action words, the guard becomes a prisoner. Choose a prisoner to replace the guard.
- After reading the story, ask preteens to use their Bibles to answer the following questions about today's study:
  - » What happened at the jail? (*a violent earthquake*, v. 26)
  - » How did the jailer react? (*He drew his sword to kill himself*, v. 27.)
  - » Who rescued the jailer? (*Paul*, v. 28)
  - » What did the jailer ask Paul and Silas? (*What must I do to be saved?* v. 30.)
  - » How did Paul and Silas answer the jailer's question? (*Believe on the Lord Jesus Christ*, v. 31.)

Prison Life

- Distribute FLYTE magazines. Direct preteens to turn to the article "Prison Life" on page 10.
- Ask a volunteer to read the "Inside the Bars" portion of the article aloud. Then allow another to read the "Outside the Bars" portion.
- Direct preteens to complete the response portion of the magazine piece. Instruct them to put an X in the "Paul and Silas" column if a statement applies to the missionaries and in the "The Jailer" column if it applies to the jailer.
- Allow preteens to read the statements and record their answers. Review the answers as a group.
- Encourage preteens to explain any answers that do not agree. In some cases, an answer might change depending on whether the reader considers the beginning or the end of the story.

The Heart of the Matter

- Prior to the session, choose either the ABC or FAITH Salvation Plan (Item 3) and read over "Sharing Your Faith" (Item 4).
- Take a few minutes to explain to preteens how they can become Christians and go to heaven someday.
- Pray with preteens who would like to make the decision to follow Christ. Affirm preteens who have already made the decision. Follow up with any preteens who are not yet ready to make the decision.

Life: World's Answer >>>

What Does the World Say?

- Direct preteens to locate "What Does the World Say?" on page 11 in their magazines.
- Review the questions and answers reflected there.
- Point out that this research is a study of responses by 12- to 19-year-olds.
- Ask preteens if they find anything odd about the answers to these questions.
- Ask them if they believe most of the people answering the questions really know the way to heaven.

Do You Know the Way?

- Ask if anyone knows how to get to a local landmark—a school, a lake, or so forth—in your community.
- Form several small groups. Give each group one of the prepared paper strips. Tell groups to not share the location written on their paper strip. If your class is smaller, give each preteen a strip of paper.
- Give each group a sheet of copy paper and tell the groups to write directions from the church to the landmark identified on their strips.
- Allow a few minutes for preteens to complete the assignment, then tell groups to give their directions (but not location strip) to another group to read.
- Encourage groups to guess where the directions would take them. Allow groups to share any corrections they feel need to be made to the directions.
- Guide preteens to locate "Directions" in the magazine (page 11).
- Discuss the various answers people provided for how to go to heaven. Ask preteens, "Do the directions for going to heaven in this section match the directions God gave in the Bible?" (*No.*)

Get Ready
- FLYTE magazine (page 11)
- strips of paper—On each strip, write the name of a different local landmark.
- copy paper

UNIT 1 HEAVEN

Get Ready
- additional paper strips from Get Started
- masking tape
- scissors

Together: My Answer >>>

What Didn't Paul and Silas Say?
- Point out that, despite what many people believe, there is really only one path to heaven.
- Ask the following questions about Acts 16:31:
  - » Did Paul and Silas say the jailer needed to belong to a certain church to be saved? (*No.*)
  - » Did they say the jailer needed to follow a lot of rules? (*No.*)
  - » Did they say everyone would be saved? (*No.*)
  - » Did they ask the jailer what sort of sins he had committed? (*No.*)
  - » Did they say it did not matter what the jailer believed? (*No.*)
- Remind preteens that what Paul and Silas did not say is nearly as important as what they did say.

Breaking Free Revisited
- Invite the preteen who performed best in the opening "Breaking Free" activity to stand in front of the group.
- Instruct him to stand with his arms at his side while you wrap twice as many paper bands as were previously broken around his arms and tape them thoroughly.
- Allow the bound preteen to attempt to break free.
- Point out this person has no way to escape.
- Show a pair of scissors and ask the preteen if he believes you can free him.
- When he agrees, carefully cut off the bands of paper.
- Emphasize that while people cannot escape the prison of sin by their own power, they can trust Jesus to set them free from sin.

Over and Out
- Dismiss preteens with these final thoughts:
  - » The way to go to heaven is not complicated.
  - » There is only one way to go to heaven.
  - » To go to heaven, a person needs to believe in the Lord Jesus Christ.
- Pray, thanking God for providing a clear and attainable way to go to heaven. Ask that God draw each preteen in the group to Himself.

DO I HAVE TO BE BAPTIZED TO GO TO HEAVEN?

Session Overview

An apparent mind-reading demonstration, a trial-based Bible study, a look at various styles of baptism, and a focus on the essentials of biblical baptism will help preteens recognize baptism as an important act of obedience but not a requirement for going to heaven.

Teacher Bible Study >>>

Ask a dozen preteens, "Have you been baptized?" In our culture, many are likely to say they have been baptized. The methods and meanings of those baptisms, however, may range widely. Baptism is not a guaranteed ticket into heaven, nor does lack of baptism bar entrance into heaven.

For centuries, people in the church have found themselves fighting about how much power should be assigned to the ordinances of the church. Doing so runs the risk of making both the Lord's Supper and baptism seem less important than they truly are. Today's Scripture passage attempts to strike a balance between those who place too much authority and power on the act of baptism and those who do not give it sufficient importance.

Luke 23:32-49 speaks against baptismal regeneration (the teaching that baptism causes salvation). The thief on the cross looked to Jesus, depended on Jesus, and received salvation from Jesus. No act of baptism was necessary to send this criminal directly to heaven.

Matthew 3:13-17, on the other hand, places proper emphasis on the importance of baptism. If Jesus insisted on being baptized to fulfill all righteousness, can you do any less? Baptism, while not essential, should be viewed as an important mark of obedience and witness. As you lead this session, walk carefully between making baptism a redeeming act and making it an unimportant piece of tradition.

Pray. Ask God to open preteens' minds to the often complicated views of baptism. Pray that those who have not accepted Christ as Savior or followed that decision with baptism would do so soon.

FLYTE Plan

Baptism is not required for entrance into heaven. This session will explore baptism as an act of obedience to God.

Bible Study
Matthew 3:13-17; Luke 23:32-49

Memory Passage
Isaiah 57:15

Level of Biblical Learning
(Salvation): When the Holy Spirit convicts me of my sin, I can trust Jesus as my personal Savior.

Get Ready
- "Heaven Session 3: Takeoff" (DVD)
- 9 equally-sized photographs

Get Started >>>

Takeoff
- Play "Heaven Session 3: Takeoff" (DVD) three minutes before the designated start time for the session.
- Allow preteens a minute or two to talk about the Weird of the Da

Pick a Picture
- Read the following instructions and practice the activity a few times before the session begins:
    - » Arrange nine equally-sized photographs on a table in three rows of three.
    - » Announce that your co-teacher can "read your mind" and wil guess which of the nine photos you have selected. Ask the co teacher to turn around. Then, show preteens which card you chose. To make the activity seem even trickier, let preteens select a photo.
    - » Point to a photo other than the one you have chosen and ask the co-teacher, "Is it this one?" Point to the part of that photo that corresponds with your chosen photo's position in the rows. For example, if your photo is the top-left one in the arrangement, point to the top-left corner of the first photo.
    - » When the co-teacher answers, "No," point to other photos. The co-teacher should be able to correctly identify the chose photo when you point to it.
- Continue this activity, switching roles.
- Allow any preteens who believe they understand the code to tak the role of the co-teacher and attempt to identify the chosen care

Join the Club
- Recognize any preteens who figured out the photo-picking code Announce that they are members of an exclusive club.
- Ask the non-club members if they feel excluded by not being in your club.
- Ask what action is required for membership in the club.
- Point out that most clubs and groups require some sort of action before a person can be a member. Allow preteens to offer some examples of how groups bring in new members: try-outs, auditions, joining ceremonies, and so forth.
- Explain that today's session will focus on baptism as an act of obedience to God.

Faith: God's Answer >>>

Before You Start

- Print the article "New Believers and Baptism" from the CD-ROM.
- Read the article and re-familiarize yourself with baptism and Jesus' command to be baptized.

What Does It Mean?

- Show the "Isaiah 57:15 Poster" and lead preteens to read it aloud.
- Ask for volunteers to read aloud the definitions of the key words from Isaiah 57:15 in the "What Does It Mean?" magazine activity.
- After each definition is read, guide a discussion about the word. Guide preteens to think of antonyms (words with opposite meanings) of the word and then think of synonyms (words with the same meaning).
- Call for volunteers to read the verse aloud from the poster, substituting the defined words with one of the synonyms they thought of.
- Ask preteens if they feel like they understand the verse better now that they know the definitions of the key words. Explain that understanding the verse is important.
- OPTION: If you've not shown it already, show "Revive" (DVD).

Study the Bible: Matthew 3:13-17; Luke 23:32-49

- Call for three volunteers to read from the Bible as follows:
  - » The first reader should locate and read Matthew 3:13-17. Before the reading, point out the context of this passage: it occurred at the very beginning of Jesus' ministry when Jesus' cousin, John the Baptist, was preaching and baptizing people at the Jordan River.
  - » The second reader should find and read Luke 23:32-38. Before this reading, explain that these events took place at the very end of Jesus' ministry, as He had been arrested and condemned to be crucified.
  - » The third reader should continue the passage from Luke, reading Luke 23:39-49. Preface this reading by explaining that it continues Luke's account of the crucifixion, focusing on a conversation Jesus had with one of the thieves crucified alongside him.
- Point out that these two passages seem to suggest different views of the necessity of baptism. Explain that this disagreement needs to be resolved in order to understand the importance of baptism in going to heaven.

The Trial

- Announce that you will be conducting a "trial" today to arrive at the answer to a very important question: Do I have to be baptized to go to heaven?

Get Ready

- "Revive (Music Video)," "Questions from You: Baptism (Feature)" (DVD)
- Items 1, 5: "Isaiah 57:15 Poster" "New Believers and Baptism" (CD-ROM)
- FLYTE magazine (page 13)

UNIT 1 HEAVEN

- Form two groups and give them the following assignments:
  - » The first group should read Matthew 3:13-17. They will represent this position: "Baptism is necessary to go to heaven."
  - » The second group should read Luke 23:39-43. They will represent this position: "Baptism is not necessary to go to heaven."
- Direct the groups to read the assigned verses in their Bibles.
- Assist them in filling in the "Trial Notes" in the magazine (page 13). Each team should record reasons for supporting its position the space allotted in the magazine.

To the Jury

- Allow the first group to present its arguments to the class. Follow this with the arguments from the second group.
- Lead a discussion, attempting to reconcile the two sides of the argument. As much as possible, allow preteens to introduce the ideas, but be sure that the following ideas are discussed:
  - » Is there a difference between what is necessary to reach heaven and what is needed "to fulfill all righteousness"?
  - » Why did John the Baptist say he needed to be baptized by Jesus? Does everyone?
  - » Could the thief have been baptized before being crucified?
  - » Is being in paradise different than going to heaven?
- Conclude the discussion by helping preteens recognize that baptism is commanded and desirable but that it is not required t go to heaven.

Do I Have To?

- Cue the DVD to "Questions from You: Baptism" and show the video.
- Debrief by reviewing the information from the video for a few minutes.

Life: World's Answer >>>

Different Methods, Different Reasons

- Ask preteens to discuss any methods of baptism that look different from what is practiced in your church.
- Point out that in order to understand the various methods and purposes of baptism, preteens need to answer three important questions:
  - » How is the baptism actually done?
  - » What is the reason given for performing baptism?
  - » Who is baptized?
- Direct preteens to consider the several different views of baptism explored in the FLYTE magazine item "Different Methods, Different Reasons" (page 14).
- Guide preteens to discuss the three above questions about baptism and to rank them in order of importance.
- Encourage them to recognize that if baptism is a symbolic act, the method of performing it—while important—is less important than the person being baptized and his or her reasons for baptism.
- Allow preteens to consider the remaining two questions to determine which is more important. Point out that since the two questions are very closely related, ranking one above the other is virtually impossible.
- Conclude this section by emphasizing that baptism is an act of obedience to Christ. It is a public display of trusting in Him as Lord and Savior. Baptism is not about tradition or doing it because your friends are being baptized. What is important is the attitude of a person's heart.

Get Ready
- FLYTE magazine (page 14)

UNIT 1 HEAVEN

Get Ready
- "Baptism Essentials (FLYTE Option)" (DVD)
- FLYTE magazine (page 15)
- photographs from Get Started

Together: My Answer >>>

Baptism Essentials

- Ask preteens to describe as many details as they can about the way baptism is practiced in your church.
- Cue the DVD to "Baptism Essentials."
- Tell preteens that they will be watching a video showing a variety of baptisms practiced all over the world.
- Ask preteens to answer these questions regarding what they expect to see:
    - » How are the people baptized? (*by immersion*)
    - » Who is being baptized? (*believers, adults and children old enough to make a decision*)
    - » Why are they being baptized? (*to symbolize their faith in Jesus and what He has done in their lives*)
- Show the video, instructing the group to watch and listen for things that seem strange as well as things that the baptisms have in common.
- Discuss the differences in these baptisms. Make note of the differences but emphasize the consistencies:
    - » All of the baptisms involved immersion.
    - » All of the people baptized were old enough to make a decision.

What If?

- Guide preteens to turn to "What If?" in the magazine (page 15).
- Discuss preteens' answers to the various case studies found there.

Join the Club

- Ask preteens if they believe that the photo-picking activity from Get Started truly proved you have mind-reading abilities.
- Reset the rows of photos and replay the activity once.
- Explain the code and allow a couple of preteens to show they understand it.
- Point out that just like this code is not magic, neither is baptism.
- Be sure to point out that baptism is far more important than this picture game.

Over and Out

- Dismiss preteens with these final thoughts:
    - » Baptism is not a magical action.
    - » Baptism of believers by immersion is an important act of obedience.
    - » Baptism is not required to go to heaven, but it is desirable.
- Pray, thanking God for salvation through Jesus, which is symbolized in baptism.

HOW CAN I HELP MY FRIENDS GO TO HEAVEN?

ession Overview

paper clip chain, a study of nine diverse Bible verses, an offended cipient of a witnessing attempt, and several video case studies will lp preteens recognize that they can and must help their friends go heaven.

eacher Bible Study >>>

od loves the world. Your calling as a Christian is to share the good ws of Jesus with the people around you. Unless evangelism comes naturally for you as breathing, there are probably many people with om you share your life who have not heard the gospel.

Do you feel inadequate as a witness? The nine verses shared in this ssion lay out several important truths.

Romans 3:23 reminds Christians that everyone has sinned, while ke 13:3 emphasizes the need to repent. The path to heaven is nple. Romans 10:9 shows another simple and clear expression of w a person can take advantage of God's amazing grace.

But it is not easy. Matthew 7:21 says that this path to heaven cannot faked. You must mean what you say, which involves acting on your lief, as seen in James 2:13.

he benefits begin today. In John 10:10, Jesus explained that He ne to give you abundant life. The benefits last for eternity. John 3 shares a marvelous promise: Jesus left His disciples for a time order to prepare a place for them. Having prepared that place, He omised to come back and bring them—and you—to be with Him. God loves people so much that He sent Jesus. How can you not pond to that love and generosity by leading friends, beginning with e preteens you teach, toward heaven?

ay. Ask God to grant boldness to the believers and to open and ten the hearts of those who have not yet believed in Jesus. Pray t boldness would begin with you.

FLYTE Plan

True friends cannot risk allowing their friends to go to hell. Christians should be links in the chain to help friends go to heaven.

Bible Study
Ephesians 1:7; John 3:16; Matthew 7:21; James 2:13; Romans 3:23; Luke 13:3; Romans 10:9; John 10:10; 14:3

Memory Passage
Isaiah 57:15

Level of Biblical Learning
(Salvation): Jesus took the punishment for everyone's sin.

Get Ready
- "Heaven Session 4: Takeoff" (DVD)
- 150 paper clips or more
- watch or timer

Get Started >>>

Takeoff
- Play "Heaven Session 4: Takeoff" (DVD) three minutes before the designated start time for the session.
- Allow preteens a minute or two to talk about the Weird of the Da

Make the Chain
- Form three equal groups of preteens. Give each group at least 5 paper clips.
- Explain that teams will have 30 seconds to assemble the longest chain of paper clips they can.
- Prompt preteens to begin. Allow the teams to work for 30 secon before directing them to stop.
- Guide the teams to stretch their chains out from a common wall.
- Compare the chains to determine which team's chain is longest.
- If your group is small, allow preteens to work by themselves. If your group is large, consider creating more than three groups.

Human Chain
- Display the longest chain to the entire group. Ask them how mu they believe this paper clip chain is worth. Point out that paper clips typically cost about one cent each.
- Challenge the teams to create a new chain, this time with peopl Direct them to start with one person touching the common wall and the remainder should join hands to stretch as far across the room as possible. If your group is small, form two teams or guid the class to form one chain.
- Give the signal to begin. When all the teams have formed their longest possible chains, ask them to compare these chains to th paper clip chains. Ask: "Which chains are worth more?"

The New Links
- Allow the human chains to be broken but instruct the groups to remain together.
- Explain that all Christians exist as links in a chain. Each believer was led to Christ by the actions of someone else, who was brought to Christ by someone else. The chain traces back throug time until it reaches the apostles, who were brought to faith by Jesus Himself.
- Ask preteens if they intend to be the last link in their chains or if they want to help bring others to heaven by adding to the chain

Faith: God's Answer >>>

Link It Up

- Instruct preteens to locate Isaiah 57:15 in their Bibles.
- Give one copy of "Isaiah 57:15 Links" (Item 6) to each of the three teams. Guide one preteen on each team to cut apart the phrases as indicated on the page.
- Distribute the phrases to the members of each team.
- Direct the teams to link up their phrases as quickly as possible to form the entire verse. Explain that they may consult their Bibles but must work from the beginning of the verse and proceed through to the end.
- Whoever has the first phrase should place it on the floor and read it aloud.
- The person holding the next phrase should add hers and read the verse so far.
- Continue in this manner until the entire verse is assembled.
- Allow all three teams to complete their verses. Then ask the class to recite the verse together.
- Review this month's unit passage by asking questions from facts they learned in "Isaiah Facts" (page 17) and definitions they learned in "What Does It Mean?" (page 23).
- OPTION: Show "Revive" (DVD).

Study the Bible: Ephesians 1:7; John 3:16; Matthew 7:21; James 2:13; Romans 3:23; Luke 13:3; Romans 10:9; John 10:10; 14:3

- Move the three teams to different areas of the room and assign them three of the verses from "Session 4 Verses" (Item 7).
- Distribute FLYTE magazines and direct preteens to the "Verses vs. Verses" questions on page 16.
- Ask the teams to read the questions and determine which three questions are best answered by their three verses.
- Read each question in turn, allowing the teams to provide their answers. Instruct a preteen from the team with the corresponding verse to stand and read the entire verse, including the Scripture reference. The correct answers are as follows:
    1. *Say, "Jesus is Lord," and believe God raised Him*; Romans 10:9
    2. *Give abundant life*, John 10:10
    3. *He sent Jesus*, John 3:16
    4. *Mercy*, James 2:13
    5. *No*, Matthew 7:21
    6. *You will perish*, Luke 13:3
    7. *His blood*, Ephesians 1:7
    8. *Us*, John 14:3
    9. *All have sinned*, Romans 3:23
- Allow time for each preteen to link the questions with the proper verses.

Get Ready

- "Revive (Music Video)" (DVD)
- Items 6, 7: "Isaiah 57:15 Links," "Session 4 Verses" (CD-ROM)
- FLYTE magazine (page 16)

Verses vs. Verses

- Point out that the Bible often seems complicated and contradictory when you do not know its teaching well enough. Provide an example:
  - » Ask the person with John 3:16 to read it aloud.
  - » Then ask the preteen holding Matthew 7:21 to read it aloud.
  - » Point out that one seems to call the other into question.
  - » Allow a period of discussion attempting to reconcile these tw verses. Point out that when the word *believe* of John 3:16 is understood correctly, there is no contradiction.
- Ask if any of the other verses seem to create similar problems, either with another verse or just popular belief.
- If the class does not suggest difficulties, consider the following:
  - » James 2:13 seems to require something beyond believing. Emphasize that believing is not a simple thing in the Bible. Believing involves depending upon something. Showing mercy when you have been shown mercy is a natural part of biblical believing.
  - » Luke 13:3 says Christians have to repent, but John 3:16 and Romans 10:9 do not say anything about repenting. Explain that part of seeing Jesus as Lord is to see ourselves as sinne If you do not repent, then you really have not seen Jesus as Lord.
- Guide the resulting discussion carefully. Should a preteen raise a question you are not prepared to answer, offer to look into the matter during the week and follow up next week.

Life: World's Answer >>>

The World in America

- Invite preteens to comment on how non-Christians might view Christians when they attempt to share their faith with them. Direct preteens to read the list of terms in the magazine article, "Don't Be Like That!" on page 17.
- Cue the DVD to "The World in America."
- Explain that the video represents international students living in America. Guide preteens to think about the students' answers in terms of what they have learned this month about heaven. Play the DVD.
- Ask preteens why they think the interviewees' beliefs are so different from theirs.

List It

- Allow a volunteer to locate and read 1 Corinthians 1:18. Point out that a negative reaction to the gospel should be expected.
- Guide the group in making a list on a whiteboard of the complaints, either stated outright or implied, that the person in the video had about Christians.
- Add any other complaints to the list that the class believes are important.
- Ask the group to categorize these complaints into three groups:
  » Things that simply aren't true, such as *Christians think they are perfect.*
  » Things that are true and can be changed, such as *Christians can be pushy.*
  » Things that are true and cannot be changed, such as *Christians believe they have the only way to go to heaven.*
- Remind preteens that resistance to Jesus as the only way to go to heaven is natural, but preteens must share the gospel anyway.

Get Ready
- "The World in America (FLYTE Option)" (DVD)
- FLYTE magazine (page 17)
- whiteboard, dry erase markers

UNIT 1 HEAVEN

Get Ready

- "How Can I Help My Friend? (Feature)" (DVD)
- FLYTE magazine (page 18)

Together: My Answer >>>

How Can I Help My Friend?

- Ask preteens if they would allow a friend to touch something extremely hot. If they would not, then how could they allow a friend to risk spending eternity in hell?
- Suggest that helping a friend go to heaven does not have to be difficult or unpleasant.
- Cue the DVD to "How Can I Help My Friend?" and tell preteens that they will watch a video that will include helps on how to tell their friends how to go to heaven.
- Play the DVD.

Adding to the Chain

- Encourage preteens to recall information they saw in the video.
- Remind preteens that Christians cannot ignore the most importa need their friends might have. Direct them to the magazine articl "Adding to the Chain" (page 18) and guide volunteers to read th article aloud, pausing to discuss after each paragraph is read.
- Direct attention to the comfort scale at the top of the page. Ask preteens to mark how comfortable they are with sharing their fait with friends.
- Help preteens know that they will become more comfortable wit sharing their faith with friends as they do it more and more.

Over and Out

- Dismiss preteens with these final thoughts:
  » You can and must help your friends go to heaven by sharing the good news of Jesus Christ's love and forgiveness.
  » Witnessing is difficult for most people.
  » If you pray and watch for opportunities, you can share Christ effectively.
- Pray, asking God to provide both courage and opportunities for preteens to help their friends go to heaven.

UNIT 2
CHANGE

Memory Passage: Psalm 71:17-18

Session 1: Why Is My Body Changing?
- Bible passage: Ecclesiastes 3:1-8; Jeremiah 1:4-10
- This session will help preteens understand God's design for their bodies.

Session 2: How Is My Body Changing?
- Bible passage: 1 Samuel 1:20-28; 2:18-26; 3:1-19; 7:13-17; 8:1-3
- Growing and changing is part of life. Preteens will learn that each person is unique and their bodies change on different timetables than their peers.

Session 3: How Can I Cope with My Changing Body?
- Bible passage: Proverbs 3:1-12
- This session is designed to help preteens know that physical maturity is a normal fact of life.

Session 4: Why Do I Care What People Think of Me?
- Bible passage: 1 Samuel 17:12-58
- This session is designed to help preteens know that they are unique and created specifically by God.

ndy Leach wrote the Change study. She is minister to children at orth Richland Hills Baptist Church in North Richland Hills, Texas.

UNIT 2 FLYTE PREP

Other FLYTE Necessities:

FLYTE DVD
The FLYTE DVD has everything you need to enhance media usage with your preteens. Take advantage of the great DVD episodes every week: a countdown clock, Weird of the Day video, teaching video, memory passage music video, and much more.

FLYTE CD-ROM
All the teacher helps, articles, and activity helps you could ever want are found on the CD-ROM. And, because it's important to keep parents in the loop, we've included parent letters for you to e-mail or mail parents (like with a stamp!) to give them a heads-up as to what you will be studying. Take time to explore the entire FLYTE CD-ROM so you don't miss something awesome.

FLYTE Learner Magazine
The FLYTE magazine for preteens is designed to really get your preteens' attention. Exciting graphics, relevant articles, and fun activities will enhance your session as well as provide a resource that preteens can take home and use for future reference. You'll want to buy one for every preteen in your class!

For updates and information, find FLYTE online at
www.lifeway.com/flyte

Session 1: Why Is My Body Changing?
You will need:
- DVD: Why Is My Body Changing? Episodes
- CD-ROM Items 8, 9, 10, 11, 12
- FLYTE magazine (pages 21-23)
- 4 large sheets of paper
- copy paper
- markers

Session 2: How Is My Body Changing?
You will need:
- DVD: How Is My Body Changing? Episodes
- CD-ROM Item 8
- FLYTE magazine (pages 24-26)
- masking tape
- index cards
- play dough

Session 3: How Can I Cope with My Changing Body?
You will need:
- DVD: How Can I Cope with My Changing Body? Episodes
- CD-ROM Items 8, 13, 14, 15
- FLYTE magazine (pages 27-29)
- balloons
- rubber bands
- copy paper
- bag of marshmallows
- 30-second timer or watch with a second hand
- colored pens or highlighting markers (two different colors)
- video camera (optional)
- large sheets of paper (optional)

Session 4: Why Do I Care What People Think of Me?
You will need:
- DVD: Why Do I Care What People Think of Me? Episodes
- CD-ROM Items 8, 16, 17, 18
- FLYTE magazine (pages 30-32)
- sticky notes
- poster board
- scissors
- glue
- markers
- table tennis balls
- department store ad or catalog of teenage girls' clothes
- sports magazines or sports pages from newspapers

WHY IS MY BODY CHANGING?

Session Overview

...fast-paced drawing game, a discussion on God's plan for change, ...comparison activity of Jeremiah, and a silly advice video will help ...eteens accept God's design for their bodies.

Teacher Bible Study >>>

...ange is part of God's design for the natural world. Time and ...asons change in predictable patterns, and spontaneous change ...ems to happen every day. Even your physical body was created to ...ow and change.

...n this week's passage, Ecclesiastes 3:1-8, Solomon contemplated ...e seasons of change and emphasized that there is an appropriate ...he for everything. Consider the passage and the ways you have ...rsonally experienced the times described. How was God at work ...ough those changing times in your life?

...Study Jeremiah 1:4-10 as a personal example of God's timing. ...fore Jeremiah was born, God chose him to be His prophet to the ...tions. As a young man, Jeremiah heard God's call, and he wasn't ...illed about the change. He made excuses, like being unable to ...eak and being too young. But God took charge, touched Jeremiah's ...outh, and Jeremiah began to speak the words of the Lord. The ...ange wasn't easy for Jeremiah, but he obediently accepted his call. ...Change will happen throughout your life. How will you trust God to ...e you through those inevitable changes?

...The preteens in your class are on the precipice of significant physical ...ange. Help them understand that change is part of God's perfect ...an and that, like Jeremiah, they can trust God to see them through.

...**ay.** Thank God for His amazing design and faithfulness in the midst ...change. Pray that each preteen you teach will understand and ...cept the changes God has in store for him or her.

FLYTE Plan

This session will help preteens understand God's design for their bodies.

Bible Study
Ecclesiastes 3:1-8;
Jeremiah 1:4-10

Memory Passage
Psalm 71:17-18

Level of Biblical Learning
(Self): I can appreciate my value as a person God loves.

Get Ready

- "Change Session 1: Takeoff," "Lameshow: How Is My Body Changing? (Feature)" (DVD)
- copy paper
- markers

Get Started >>>

Takeoff

- Play "Change Session 1: Takeoff" (DVD) three minutes before the designated start time for the session.
- Allow preteens a minute or two to talk about the Weird of the Da

Play a Drawing Game

- Form groups of three or four preteens.
- Instruct groups to sit with their backs to each other.
- Give each group a piece of copy paper and a few markers.
- Explain that each group will work together to draw a face using the following rules:
  » Only one preteen at a time may see the paper and draw.
  » Teams may not communicate with each other by talking or a other communication method.
  » Each time you say "change," the preteen with the paper will immediately pass it to the group member on his right, who will continue the drawing.
- Begin the game. Say "change" at various time intervals to keep the activity challenging.
- Continue play for several minutes. Encourage preteens to add more detail and continue taking turns as directed.
- Correct any groups who try to talk with each other or peek.
- End the game by instructing preteens to turn their papers over.
- Invite groups to share their completed faces with the other groups.

Talk About It

- Discuss the following questions:
  » What would have made this game easier for you?
  » How easy was it for you to envision the finished drawing?
  » What was frustrating about this activity?
- Explain that, like the drawings changed throughout the game, th world God created is full of things that change.
- Invite preteens to identify some things in creation that change. (For example, seasons, weather, caterpillars, trees, people.)
- Explain that change is part of God's plan, and God's plans are good.

Lameshow: How Is My Body Changing?

- Play "Lameshow: How Is My Body Changing?" from the DVD.
- Briefly discuss the silly answers given during the video explainin how a body changes.
- Announce that today preteens will take a serious look at God's plan for change.

Faith: God's Answer >>>

Memory Passage: Psalm 71:17-18

- Display the "Psalm 71:17-18 Poster" (Item 8) and guide preteens to recite the passage in unison.
- Encourage preteens to memorize Psalm 71:17-18 during this unit.
- Call attention to the phrases *from my youth* and *even when I am old and gray*. Explain that God designed people to age and that many changes happen over the course of a person's life.
- Form three groups and assign each group one phrase from the passage to say aloud.
- Guide each group to stand as they recite their portion of the verse.
- Change assignments and recite the verse several more times.
- OPTION: Cue the DVD to "Another Generation" and play the music video.

Study the Bible: Ecclesiastes 3:1-8

- Tell preteens to open their Bibles to Ecclesiastes 3:1-8.
- Invite a volunteer to read the passage aloud as the class follows along.
- Point out that each phrase in the passage contains an opposite.
- Ask preteens to identify some of the times described and to give a modern example of what that might look like. (For example, a time to tear down; imploding a dilapidated building.)
- Explain that the passage is a reminder that change happens throughout life and different responses are appropriate as situations change.
- Give each preteen one "A Time To … " card from the CD-ROM. Instruct preteens to use their Bibles to find each corresponding opposite and find the person who is holding that card.
- Tell the pairs to work together and complete "Modern Times" in their FLYTE magazines (page 22).
- Invite pairs to share their modern times statements.
- Note: If your group is small, give each preteen a card and then ask him to pull the opposite card from a pile. Complete "Modern Times" as a group.

Discuss Change

- Remind preteens of some of the creation changes they identified during Get Started.
- Discuss the following questions:
  - » What changes are taking place among kids your age? (*new school, different hobbies and interests, clothing styles*)
  - » What physical changes have you noticed happening with your friends? (*getting taller, hair styles, voice changing*)
- Explain that the preteen years are a time of significant physical change as bodies transition from childhood to adulthood.
- Tell preteens that this month they will learn what they can expect

Get Ready
- "Another Generation (Music Video)" (DVD)
- Items 8, 9: "Psalm 71:17-18 Poster," "'A Time To …' Cards" (CD-ROM)
- FLYTE magazine (pages 21, 22)

UNIT 2 CHANGE

as their bodies change, how to handle the change in a way that is pleasing to God, and that God designed their bodies to undergo physical changes.

Study a Bible Example: Jeremiah 1:4-10

- Tell preteens to find Jeremiah 1:4-10 in their Bibles.
- Guide them to open their FLYTE magazines to "Jeremiah's Call" (page 21).
- Explain that the passage tells how God called Jeremiah to be a prophet who would boldly speak God's words to the people.
- As preteens complete each section of the magazine activity, ask two volunteers to read the sections of verses aloud.
- Lead preteens to discuss the questions about that portion of the passage.

What About Me?

- As preteens reflect on the life of Jeremiah, lead them to discuss the following questions:
    » What was God's plan for Jeremiah? What is His plan for you?
    » When did God choose Jeremiah for this task? When did God choose you?
    » What did God want Jeremiah to do? What does God want you to do?
    » What excuses did Jeremiah make? What excuses might you be making?
    » What promises did God make to Jeremiah? What promises has God made to you?
- Help the students understand that God faithfully keeps His promises and that they can trust God as they undergo changes in their lives.

Trust Prayer Letters

- Instruct preteens to complete "Trust Prayer Letters" in the FLYTE magazine (page 22). You may want to play soft music while they work.
- When preteens finish writing their letters, guide each preteen to read his letter silently as a prayer to God.

Life: World's Answer >>>

Don't Take My Word for It

- Tell preteens they will have the opportunity to offer some really bad advice!
- Form four groups of preteens and give each group a sheet of paper and one of the strips from "Don't Take My Word for It."
- Instruct each group to read the scenario and then write several bad responses people might give to answer the preteen's question.
- Allow groups to share their scenarios and advice.
- Explain that the answers the world offers are not always best. Sometimes the world is cruel and uncaring.

Transition

- Form separate groups of boys and girls for the remainder of today's session.

For Girls Only

- Read the list of common questions girls ask.
- Explain that many girls look for answers by asking friends or searching the Internet, which may not give accurate information or complete answers. Some girls never look for answers because they are embarrassed or think they're the only ones with that question.
- Help preteens identify places they can find correct information and answers to their questions. (For example, parents, trusted adults, Christian books, and so forth.)
- Remind girls that the Bible offers solutions to many of life's biggest challenges.

For Guys Only

- Read the list of common questions guys ask.
- Explain that many boys look for answers by asking friends or searching the Internet, which may not give accurate information or complete answers. Some boys never look for answers because they are embarrassed or think they're the only ones with that question.
- Help boys identify places they can find correct information and answers to their questions. (For example, parents, trusted adults, Christian books, and so forth.)
- Remind boys that the Bible offers solutions to many of life's biggest challenges.

Get Ready
- Item 10: "Don't Take My Word for It" (CD-ROM)
- 4 large sheets of paper

Get Ready: Girls Only
- Item 11: "Common Questions Girls Ask" (CD-ROM)

Get Ready: Guys Only
- Item 12: "Common Questions Guys Ask" (CD-ROM)

UNIT 2 CHANGE

Get Ready: Girls Only
- Item 10: "Don't Take My Word for It" (CD-ROM)
- FLYTE magazine (page 23)

Get Ready: Guys Only
- Item 10: "Don't Take My Word for It" (CD-ROM)
- FLYTE magazine (page 23)

Together: My Answer >>>

For Girls Only
- Guide girls to use their Bibles to complete "Advice Match-Up" in the FLYTE magazine (page 23).
- Reinforce God's Word as the best source of advice for all kinds of situations.
- Form groups of three or four girls and explain that the groups will produce their own radio broadcasts using God's Word as the source of good advice.
- Guide groups to choose a problem and biblical solution from "Advice Match-Up" to create their broadcasts.
- Groups will present their completed broadcasts to the other groups of girls.
- Remind girls of the "Don't Take My Word for It" activity. Ask them to think of advice to give the preteens from the scenarios that a trusted Christian friend might give.

For Guys Only
- Guide boys to use their Bibles to complete "Advice Match-Up" in the FLYTE magazine (page 23).
- Reinforce God's Word as the best source of advice for all kinds of problems.
- Form groups of three or four boys and explain that the groups will produce their own radio broadcasts using God's Word as the source of good advice.
- Guide groups to choose a problem and biblical solution from "Advice Match-Up" to create their broadcasts.
- Groups will present their completed broadcasts to the other groups of boys.
- Remind boys of the "Don't Take My Word for It" activity. Ask the to think of advice to give the preteens from the scenarios that a trusted Christian friend might give.

Over and Out
- Dismiss both boys and girls with these final thoughts:
  » Growing from childhood to adulthood is part of God's plan f preteens' bodies. That plan for growth involves many physic changes.
  » Like Jeremiah, God has a unique plan for each of them, whic was in place before they were born.
- Remind preteens that their parents or other trusted adults are the best source for advice and information about their changing bodies.
- Lead a time of prayer. Thank God for uniquely creating each preteen. Thank Him for keeping His promise to be with them as they go through change, including physical change.

HOW IS MY BODY CHANGING?

Session Overview

n energetic exercise routine, a study of God's plan for Samuel, and
informative video will help preteens understand what to expect and
ow to trust God as their bodies change and grow.

Teacher Bible Study >>>

ow can an entire lifetime be summed up in a few short passages?
Samuel's story begn before he was even born. In 1 Samuel 1:20-28,
od answered barren Hannah's prayer by giving her a son, Samuel.
s soon as Samuel was old enough, Hannah showed her gratitude to
od by giving Samuel to Him to serve in the temple for his entire life.
Read 1 Samuel 2:18-26 to get a glimpse of Samuel's childhood
the temple. Samuel grew up in the presence of the Lord (v. 21).
magine how that must have shaped Samuel's heart. Verse 26 explains
ow Samuel grew in stature and in favor with the Lord and men. Read
ke 2:52 and compare Samuel's growth with how Jesus grew.
1 Samuel 3:1-19 gives a detailed account of the Lord speaking
Samuel. Samuel heard God and obediently delivered a difficult
essage to the priest, Eli. Verse 19 explains that as Samuel grew, the
rd was with him.
As an adult, Samuel judged Israel (1 Samuel 7:13-17) and when
muel grew old, he appointed his sons to serve in his place
Samuel 8:1-3).
A lifetime dedicated to God is truly a gift. The preteens you teach
e at the beginning of their lives. How will you impact them to grow
in God's presence and trust God their entire lives?

ay. Thank God for the way He has worked in your life, regardless of
en you began your journey of faith. Ask God to help the preteens
u teach love and trust Him for their lifetimes.

FLYTE Plan

*Growing and changing is part
of life. Preteens will learn that
each person is unique and their
bodies change at different rates.*

Bible Study
1 Samuel 1:20-28; 2:18-26;
3:1-19; 7:13-17; 8:1-3

Memory Passage
Psalm 71:17-18

Level of Biblical Learning
(Self): I can appreciate my value
as a person God loves.

Get Ready
- "Change Session 2: Takeoff" (DVD)
- masking tape—Create two lines long enough to accommodate preteen boys standing on one and preteen girls on the other.

Get Started >>>

Takeoff

- Play "Change Session 2: Takeoff" (DVD) three minutes before the designated start time for the session.
- Allow preteens a minute or two to talk about the Weird of the Da

Welcome Preteens

- As preteens arrive, explain that today's session will begin with an intense workout.
- Invite preteens to do some stretches to get ready for a coordination challenge.
- Encourage students who may be physically unable to participate to do as much as possible and cheer on the other preteens durin the activity.

Coordination Challenge

- Call attention to the masking tape lines on the floor. Guide the boys to stand on one line and girls to stand on the other. If your group is small, ask all preteens to stand on the same line.
- Tell the preteens that the goal of the challenge is to reverse the order in which they are standing. The preteen at the end of the line must be at the front and so forth by the end of the challenge
- Explain that only one person's foot may be off the line at any time That means that only one person can move at a time and it will take careful coordination to complete the challenge.
- If time allows, encourage preteens to complete the coordination challenge several times.

Debrief

- Debrief by asking the following questions:
  - » Could a baby do the challenge you just completed?
  - » Could an elderly person complete the challenge?
  - » What about a person with a broken foot?
- Explain that over the course of a lifetime, preteens' bodies will g through many changes. They couldn't do the things they can do today when they were younger. When they are older, they will be able to do things they can't do now. Affirm that these changes ar part of God's design.

Faith: God's Answer >>>

Study the Bible: 1 Samuel 1:20-28, 2:18-26, 3:1-19, 7:13-15, 8:1-3

- Explain that today's Bible study is about Samuel and events throughout his lifetime.
- Form four groups and assign the following passages:
  - » Group 1: 1 Samuel 1:20-28
  - » Group 2: 1 Samuel 2:18-26
  - » Group 3: 1 Samuel 3:1-19
  - » Group 4: 1 Samuel 7:13–8:3
- Groups should study their assigned passages and answer the following questions:
  - » About how old was Samuel in the passage?
  - » What happened to Samuel?
  - » What does the passage say about Samuel's relationship with God?

Group Reports

- Guide preteens to follow along in their Bibles as each group reports. Make the following observations after each report:
  - » Group 1: Point out verse 28. Explain that Samuel's mother was so thankful God gave her a child that she gave her son to serve God for his entire life.
  - » Group 2: Call attention to verse 21. Reinforce that Samuel grew up in the temple in God's presence. Guide preteens to read verse 26 and describe the ways Samuel grew. Compare how Samuel's growth is described in 1 Samuel 2:26 with how Jesus' growth is described in Luke 2:52.
  - » Group 3: Explain that even as a child, Samuel heard the Lord's voice and was obedient to Him. Point out verse 19. Explain that the Lord was still with Samuel as he continued to grow.
  - » Group 4: Explain that from childhood, Samuel was chosen by God. He faithfully judged Israel throughout his life (v. 15) and when he was old, he appointed his sons as judges. Samuel's sons did not walk with God faithfully like Samuel did.
- Additional information can be found in "Samuel: This Is Your Life" on page 24 in the FLYTE magazine.
- OPTION: Play the FLYTE Option: "Samuel Responds to God" (DVD).

Maturity Morph

- Guide preteens to discuss what types of physical changes Samuel might have undergone in the portions of his lifetime they studied. (*infancy, early childhood, childhood, adulthood, senior adulthood*)
- Direct preteens to "Maturity Morph" (page 26) in their magazines.
- Ask preteens to write their guess for the age of the person in each photo. (*6 months, 6 years, 12 years, 18 years, 60 years*)

Get Ready
- "Another Generation (Music Video)," "Samuel Responds to God (FLYTE Option)" (DVD)
- Item 8: "Psalm 71:17-18 Poster" (CD-ROM)
- FLYTE magazine (pages 24, 26)

- Remind preteens that the physical changes that take place during a lifetime are part of God's plan.

Memory Passage: Psalm 71:17-18

- Display the memory passage poster and guide preteens to read the passage aloud in unison.
- OPTION: Cue the DVD to "Another Generation" and play the music video.
- Invite preteens to identify the life stages in the memory passage.
- Ask preteens to apply the passage to Samuel's life by answering the following questions:
  - » How was Samuel taught by God from his youth?
  - » How did Samuel proclaim God's wonderful works?
  - » Did God abandon Samuel when he was old?
  - » How did Samuel proclaim God's power to another generation?
- Ask preteens to apply the passage to themselves by answering these questions:
  - » How have you been taught about God from your youth?
  - » How can you proclaim God's wonderful works?
  - » Will God abandon you when you are old?
  - » How can you proclaim God's power to another generation?
- Encourage preteens to commit the passage to memory.

Pray

- Explain that, like Samuel, God has a plan for each preteen's life, and He will be with them for their whole lifetimes.
- Explain that God's plans involve change and growth. Remind preteens that because God never changes, preteens can trust Him to see them through any changes that may come.
- Guide each preteen to find a partner and pray for each other to trust God in the face of change.

Life: World's Answer >>>

EACHER TIP: If you feel a little awkward when you discuss this sensitive content, then ·ngratulations—you're normal! If you appear uncomfortable discussing this content in ·ass, preteens will probably feel uncomfortable too. So speak with confidence and use ·rrect terminology.

What's Happening to Me?

- Tell preteens they are going to hear a story about a silly family called the Rocks. Play "The Rocks: What's Happening to Me?" from the DVD.
- Lead preteens to discuss the changes Rocklet and Cellula experienced.
- Form gender-specific groups for the remainder of the session.

or Girls Only

- Explain that girls' bodies will change during this time in their lives. These changes include the following:
  - » Breasts develop
  - » Hair grows on legs, under arms, and genitals
  - » Menstrual periods begin
  - » Pelvis widens and hips curve
- Emphasize that physical changes are part of God's plan for their growth.
- Give each girl some index cards and a pencil. Encourage girls to write down questions they may have about their changing bodies. Explain that questions will remain anonymous and you will do your best to answer them.
- Read and answer questions as time allows.
- Encourage girls to talk with their parents. Emphasize that parents or other trusted adults are the best source for accurate information about physical changes.

or Guys Only

- Explain that guys' bodies will change during this time in their lives. These changes include the following:
  - » Voice deepens
  - » Hair grows on your face, underarms, and genitals
  - » Muscles grow larger and become harder
  - » Penis grows bigger and changes
- Emphasize that physical changes are part of God's plan for their growth.
- Give each boy some index cards and a pencil. Encourage boys to write down questions they may have about their changing bodies. Explain that questions will remain anonymous and you will do your best to answer them.
- Read and answer questions as time allows.
- Encourage guys to talk with their parents. Emphasize that parents or other trusted adults are the best source for accurate information about physical changes.

Get Ready
- "The Rocks: What's Happening to Me? (Feature)" (DVD)

Get Ready: Girls Only
- index cards

Get Ready: Guys Only
- index cards

TEACHER TIP: As you begin to answer the questions preteens submitted, carefully screen them for group appropriateness. **DO NOT READ OR ANSWER INAPPROPRIATE OR SENSITIVE QUESTIONS**. Answer questions as simply, honestly, and accurately as possible.

UNIT 2 CHANGE

Get Ready
• FLYTE magazine (page 25)
• play dough

Together: My Answer >>>

For Girls Only and For Boys Only
• Boys and girls groups should remain separated, but they will complete the same activity.

Play Dough Creations
• Give each preteen a ball of play dough and instruct him or her to design a new animal species.
• As preteens work, continue answering questions and clarifying questions from the Life section as needed.
• After a few minutes, tell preteens to stop working for a moment and complete the following:
  » Identify unique elements of each animal's design.
  » Compare how some animals are still developing and others are more complete.
• Allow preteens to continue molding aliens for a few more minute
• Encourage preteens to tell the group about their completed animals.
• Explain that each animal developed at a different rate and is a unique creation.

Debrief
• Help preteens understand that each of them is uniquely designe by God and develops physically at a different rate.
• Encourage them that even if their bodies have not begun to change and their friends' have, it's OK.
• Call attention to "Cling to Truth" in the FLYTE magazine (page 2
• Ask volunteers to read each verse aloud.
• Instruct preteens to circle the verses that will be most helpful to them during this time of significant physical change.
• Remind them that they should stay close to God and let Him guide them throughout their lives.

Over and Out
• Dismiss preteens with these final thoughts:
  » God will be with you throughout a lifetime of changes.
  » God uniquely created you and loves you.
  » His plans for you are perfect.
  » When change happens, remember that God remains the same.
• Pray that preteens will understand that God's plan for people is to grow and change. Pray that preteens will be comfortable with God's plan for their changing bodies.

HOW CAN I COPE WITH MY CHANGING BODY?

Session Overview

A quick change balloon game, an in-depth look at wisdom from the book of Proverbs, and evaluating product advertisements will give preteens tools to cope with their changing bodies.

Teacher Bible Study >>>

Think of all the changes you've experienced in your lifetime. Some life changes are major: a new job, the birth of a child, a move. Some changes are less significant: a new haircut, traffic detours, a different brand of toothpaste. Major or minor, how can you cope with change?

Acknowledge that God never changes, and His Word remains the same. Proverbs 3:1-12 contains important truths that can help you and the preteens you teach cope with change by trusting God and living obediently. Each set of two verses contains a command from God and a promised result for obedience.

For example, look at verses 1-2. The commands: Don't forget my teaching and let your heart keep my commands. The promised result: they will bring you many days, a full life, and well-being.

As you meditate on the passage, make a list of the commands given and the promised results. Ask God to reveal to you areas in which you can improve your obedience to His commands. Choose to live obediently and claim the promised result.

The preteens you teach are in a period of radical physical change. God's Word can be a valuable tool to help them cope. As you reflect on ways God has brought you through changes in your past, allow God to use your personal experience and testimony of dependence on Him to impact the preteens you teach.

Pray. Talk to God about the preteens in your class. Pray that they would learn to cope with their changing bodies by depending on God and trusting His Word.

FLYTE Plan

This session is designed to help preteens know that physical maturity is a normal fact of life.

Bible Study
Proverbs 3:1-12

Memory Passage
Psalm 71:17-18

Level of Biblical Learning
(Self): God expects me to remain pure in all aspects of my life.

Get Ready
- "Change Session 3: Takeoff" (DVD)
- balloons
- rubber bands

Get Started >>>

Takeoff
- Play "Change Session 3: Takeoff" (DVD) three minutes before the designated start time for the session.
- Allow preteens a minute or two to talk about the Weird of the Day

Tap, Tap, Tap
- Give each preteen a balloon and instruct him to inflate it and tie a knot at the end.
- Explain that preteens will simply tap their balloons in the air, seeing who can keep his balloon up in the air the longest by tapping.
- Guide each preteen to count the number of taps. Each time the balloon touches the floor, he should begin counting again and try to improve his previous score.

Change It Up
- Frequently change the game instructions by announcing the following or creating your own changes:
    » Change that … I forgot to tell you to tap the balloon while standing on one foot.
    » Change that … You are supposed to use a rubber band to hold your wrists together while tapping.
    » Change that … You need to find a partner and tap one balloon together.
    » Change that … You must sing the national anthem while tapping your balloon.
    » Change that … Don't stand on one foot. Tap the balloon with your foot.
    » Change that … Tap the balloon while closing your eyes.
- Continue making new changes, changing things back or adding your own changes.
- After several consecutive changes, preteens should be confused and frustrated.
- Tell them to stop tapping after a few minutes have passed.
- Identify the preteen with the highest number of taps and congratulate him or her.

Debrief
- Ask preteens the following questions:
    » How hard was it to deal with all the changes to the rules?
    » What are some changes that happen in the lives of preteens?
    » How hard is it to deal with those changes?
- Explain that coping with change can be difficult, but today's session will give them some tools for coping with change.

Faith: God's Answer >>>

Study the Bible: Proverbs 3:1-12

- Direct attention to "Promises in Proverbs" on page 27 of the magazine. Provide colored pens or highlighting markers and challenge preteens to complete the activity.
- Explain that the Book of Proverbs contains wise sayings that were written and collected by King Solomon.
- Discuss the difference between wisdom and knowledge.
- Explain that wisdom is the ability to see people and situations through God's eyes and make right decisions. Knowledge is about facts, like states and capitals or long division.
- Guide preteens to find Proverbs 3:1-12 in their Bibles. Explain that this particular passage is written in couplets, or two verses that make a complete thought together. Generally, the odd verses give a command and the even verses tell the promised result.
- Form six groups of preteens. Assign two verses of the passage to each group (vv. 1-2; vv. 3-4; and so on). Groups should study their assigned verses to identify the commands given and the promised results. Direct groups to share their answers. If your group is small, complete the activity together as a large group.
- Instruct preteens to use the information shared to complete "You Do/God Will" on page 28 of the FLYTE magazine.

Discuss

- Call attention to verses 5-6 and ask the following questions:
  » In what ways do you rely on your own understanding?
  » Whom should you trust? Why?
- Call attention to verses 7-8 and ask the following questions:
  » What commands can you follow that will help keep your body healthy and strong?
  » How can turning away from evil protect your body?
- Call attention to verse 9 and ask the following questions:
  » How is your body a possession?
  » How can you honor God with your body?

Memory Passage: Psalm 71:17-18

- Cue the DVD to "Another Generation" and play the music video.
- Draw preteens' attention to the "Psalm 71:17-18 Poster" (Item 8) and guide preteens to recite the passage in unison.
- Explain that one of God's most wonderful works is the amazing human body. Guide preteens to share interesting facts they may know about the body.
- Invite preteens to look at "The Amazing Human Body" in the FLYTE magazine (page 28).
- Ask a volunteer to read one of the amazing facts aloud.
- Remind preteens that not only are their bodies amazing, each of them is uniquely created. For example, no two of them have the

Get Ready
- "Another Generation (Music Video)," "Coping Tips from David and Sissy (Feature)" (DVD)
- Item 8: "Psalm 71:17-18 Poster" (CD-ROM)
- FLYTE magazine (pages 27, 28)
- colored pens or highlighting markers (two different colors)

UNIT 2 CHANGE

same fingerprint or DNA, even if they are twins. Emphasize that every person who has ever lived is a uniquely created person who is loved by God.
- Tell preteens that knowing they are uniquely created by a loving God can give them hope and help them cope with the process of changing from children to adults.

God Is a Loving Father
- Guide preteens to read Proverbs 3:12.
- Remind them that not only are they uniquely created by God, but that God is a loving Father. Ask preteens to describe how a loving father treats his children.
- Help each preteen understand that no matter what his or her father on earth is like, God is delighted by His sons and daughters. Explain that knowing that God delights in them can give them confidence to face the future and trust God with the end result.

Coping Tips from David and Sissy
- Cue the DVD to "Coping Tips from David and Sissy."
- Tell preteens they will watch a video of two people who work with preteens. David Thomas and Sissy Goff are Christian counselors who help preteens and teens deal with life issues every day. They have great insight that will help preteens know how to cope with their changing bodies.
- Play the DVD.
- Ask preteens to identify the tools David and Sissy suggested for coping with change.

Transition
- Pray with the group, thanking God for wisdom and help to cope with change.
- Form separate groups of boys and girls for the remaining portions of today's session.

Life: World's Answer >>>

For Girls Only

- Show girls the "Amazing New Products for Girls" (Item 13).
- Discuss the promises each product makes and ask the following questions:
    - » What real products can you think of that make promises like these?
    - » Why do you think products like these are appealing to many preteens?
- Explain that using a product or taking a pill are ways many people try to cope with their changing bodies.
- Ask girls to share some other unhealthy coping methods that girls might try. (For example, extreme dieting and exercise, surgery, overeating, and so forth.)
- Discuss what might cause a girl to take extreme measures like these.
- Explain that the world's coping methods may make your body look better for a while, but they can cause serious long-term problems, and they don't address the underlying emotional issues that cause people to take these extreme measures in the first place.

For Guys Only

- Show boys the "Amazing New Products for Guys" (Item 14).
- Discuss the promises each product makes and ask the following questions:
    - » What real products can you think of that make promises like these?
    - » Why do you think products like these are marketed to preteens?
- Explain that using a product or taking a pill are ways many people try to cope with their changing bodies.
- Ask the guys to share some other unhealthy coping methods that people may try. (For example, extreme dieting and exercise, surgery, performance enhancing drugs, and so forth.)
- Discuss what might cause a guy to take extreme measures like these.
- Explain that the world's coping methods may make your body look better for a while, but they may cause serious long-term problems, and they don't help with the underlying emotional issues that cause people to take these extreme measures in the first place.

Get Ready: Girls Only
- Item 13: "Amazing New Products for Girls" (CD-ROM)

Get Ready: Guys Only
- Item 14: "Amazing New Products for Guys" (CD-ROM)

TIP: If you discover that a preteen is using unhealthy coping methods, tell a minister or pastor. Explain your concerns based on what the preteen said in class, and allow them to take appropriate action.

UNIT 2 CHANGE

Get Ready - Girls Only
- FLYTE magazine (page 29)
- copy paper
- video camera (optional)
- large sheets of paper (optional)

Get Ready - Guys Only
- Item 15: "Marshmallow Dare Cards" (CD-ROM)
- FLYTE magazine (page 29)
- bag of marshmallows (not mini-marshmallows)
- 30-second timer or watch with a second hand

Together: My Answer >>>

For Girls Only
- Invite girls to read "Ways to Cope" in the FLYTE magazine (page 29) and discuss the healthy coping strategies.
- Form two teams and distribute a piece of copy paper to each team. Give teams one minute to list physical characteristics with which girls might struggle to cope. (For example: acne, breast development, menstrual period, weight.)
- Guide teams to compare their lists.
- Instruct the teams to create a 30-second commercial advertisement for God's Word as a way for preteen girls to cope with one of the problems they listed. Encourage them to refer to "Ways to Cope" in the FLYTE magazine. If your group is shy about acting, ask them to design a billboard using large sheets of paper.
- Use a video camera to record each group's commercial.
- Allow the groups to watch the recorded videos.
- Help girls remember that they should seek godly advice and counsel when they are struggling to cope with physical changes.

For Guys Only
- Invite boys to read "Ways to Cope" in the FLYTE magazine (page 29) and discuss the healthy coping strategies.
- Place the "Marshmallow Dare Cards" facedown on the table.
- Explain that each card contains a typical boy problem.
- Boys will take turns drawing a card, identifying the correct way to cope with that problem, and completing the marshmallow dare.
- Dares must be completed within 30 seconds.
- Clarify that only the boy with the card should complete the dare.
- When all cards are used, mix them up and repeat as time allows.
- Help boys remember that they should seek godly advice and counsel when they are struggling to cope with physical changes.

Over and Out
- Remind preteens that God has a plan for their physical development, and God's Word contains wisdom to help them cope.
- Pray, thanking God for His perfect plan and asking Him to help preteens during this season of physical change.

WHY DO I CARE ABOUT WHAT PEOPLE THINK?

Session Overview

Through a photographic activity, a real-situation video, and an in-depth study of David's encounter with Goliath, preteens will learn that man looks at outward appearance, but God looks at the heart.

Teacher Bible Study >>>

When you stand in front of a mirror, what do you see? Like me, you probably notice every flaw and imperfection. It's impossible to measure up to beauty according to today's culture. But God looks at the heart. So why do I care so much about what others think of me?

Read 1 Samuel 16 for some background. Based on looks, Samuel was certain Eliab would be chosen as king. As the baby brother, David was likely compared to Eliab. Like Eliab, young David was handsome, but God noticed his heart. When David was anointed king, something significant happened. The spirit of the Lord took control of David.

Reflect on the following questions:
- What does God see when He looks at your heart?
- How have you given God's Spirit control?
- How has that affected your response to what others think of your appearance?

Read 1 Samuel 17. Notice the opinions about David. Eliab accused David of arrogance. King Saul said David was "just a youth." Goliath despised David for being healthy and handsome. Still David believed God and trusted Him to bring victory.

As their bodies change, the preteens in your class are becoming more aware of what others think about their physical appearance. They need to understand that God has a plan for their physical growth, but He is most interested in the way their hearts look.

Pray. Ask forgiveness for times you care more about your outward appearance than your heart. Give God control of this week's session.

FLYTE Plan

This session is designed to help preteens know that they are unique and created specifically by God.

Bible Study
1 Samuel 17:12-58

Memory Passage
Psalm 71:17-18

Level of Biblical Learning
(Self): My self-control and obedience to God can help me stand up to peer pressure. My self-control honors God and benefits me.

Get Ready

- "Change Session 4: Takeoff" (DVD)
- Item 16: "What Do You Think About Me? Pictures" (CD-ROM)—Post pictures around the room.
- Item 17: "Discover the Real Me" (CD-ROM)—Cut statements apart.
- sticky notes

Get Started >>>

Takeoff

- Play "Change Session 4: Takeoff" (DVD) three minutes before the designated start time for the session.
- Allow preteens a minute or two to talk about the Weird of the Day.

What Do You Think About Me?

- Give each preteen a few sticky notes and a pencil.
- Draw attention to the pictures you posted around the room. Ask preteens to draw conclusions about the people in the pictures based solely on their outward appearance.
- Guide them to move around the room and write a word or short phrase that describes their thoughts about each person and place the sticky note next to that person's picture.
- As time permits, preteens may continue adding more sticky notes to the pictures.

Discover the Real Me

- Direct preteens to form groups by choosing a picture to stand beside.
- Guide groups to share a brief description of the person in their picture and read aloud some of the words and phrases on the sticky notes placed around the picture.
- Give groups the corresponding "Discover the Real Me" statements.
- Instruct groups to read the statements aloud to the class.
- Compare and contrast the first impressions with the true statements.
- Continue until all groups have shared.

From the Outside In

- Explain that judging people based on outward appearance is common.
- Discuss how preteens judged the people in the pictures based on their outward appearances.
- Tell preteens that caring what people think about their outward appearances is a normal part of growing up, especially during the preteen years when everyone grows and changes so quickly.
- Explain that today's session will help them learn ways to deal with what others may think about the changes taking place in their outer appearances.

Faith: God's Answer >>>

What's Going On With My Body?
- Cue the DVD to "What's Going On With My Body?"
- Explain that the video shows some writing about what people think about physical appearance.
- Use the following questions to discuss the video:
  » What were some of the ideas the narrator had about physical appearance?
  » How does Scripture apply to issues that you may have with your physical appearance?
  » What does God think about your physical appearance?
- Tell preteens to think about the following questions but to not answer them aloud:
  » What do you think people say about your appearance?
  » How does that affect you?

Study the Bible: 1 Samuel 17:12-58
- Direct preteens to find 1 Samuel 17:12-58 in their Bibles.
- Explain that the story of David and Goliath is a well-known Bible story. Invite preteens to share what they know about David and Goliath. Correct any misinformation.
- Guide preteens to use their Bibles to complete "David and Goliath" on pages 30 and 31 in the FLYTE magazine.

Opinions About David
- After discussing the key portions of the story, distribute the "Opinions About David" charts. Form groups to search the Scriptures and find the following persons: Jesse, David's brothers, King Saul, Goliath. Assign each group one or more persons.
- After a few minutes, invite the groups to share. Direct preteens to complete their charts as each group reports.
- Guide preteens to identify any similarities that may have surfaced as each group shared.
- Explain that most of the opinions about David were based on his outward appearance.

What Did God Think?
- Draw preteens' attention to the "God" column on the worksheets.
- Explain that before David fought Goliath, the prophet Samuel anointed David as the next King of Israel. At that time, God spoke to Samuel.
- Guide preteens to read 1 Samuel 16:7 and identify what God said to Samuel. Tell preteens to keep this verse in mind as they complete their work.
- Discuss the following questions:
  » How much do you think David cared about what others thought of him?

Get Ready
- "Another Generation (Music Video)," "What's Going On With My Body? (Feature)" (DVD)
- Item 8: "Psalm 71:17-18 Poster" (CD-ROM)
- Item 18: "Opinions About David" (CD-ROM)—Provide one copy for each student.
- FLYTE magazine (pages 30-32)

UNIT 2 CHANGE

» How much do you think David cared about what God thought of him?
- Explain the following points:
  » David was secure in what he knew about himself—God had chosen him to be the future king, and he had killed animals before.
  » David was most secure in who he knew God to be—God had the power to rescue him from Goliath. God had been faithful to protect him in the past, and God could win the battle.

Memory Passage: Psalm 71:17-18
- Draw attention to the "Psalm 71:17-18 Poster" (Item 8).
- Give special attention to the phrase, "I still proclaim Your wonderful works."
- Cover the poster and invite preteens to recite the passage from memory.
- Ask preteens to proclaim some of God's wonderful works or tell what God has done.
- Explain that remembering the wonderful things God has done can help them find security in who God is.
- OPTION: Cue the DVD to "Another Generation" and play the music video.

Who I Am/Who God Is
- Instruct preteens to complete "Who I Am/Who God Is" in the FLYTE magazine (page 32).
- Invite volunteers to share their responses.
- Explain that, like David, preteens can be secure in the person God created them to be, but more than that, they can find their security in who God is.
- Lead a time of prayer, trusting God for who He created each preteen to be. Ask God to help preteens find their security in Him.

Transition
- Form separate groups of boys and girls for the remaining portions of today's session.

For Girls Only

- Show the girls the ad pages and supplies.
- Guide them to cut out pictures that show what the world says a girl should look like on the outside and to glue them onto the poster board to make a collage.
- Pose the following questions for discussion as the girls work:
  - » How do you think these photos might have been touched up to make them so perfect?
  - » How many kids at your school look like the girls in these pictures?
  - » What is it about these girls that the world considers beautiful?
- Discuss whether the pictures of people in magazines and on TV accurately portray the way people look in real life.
- Guide girls to compare the pictures in "What's the Difference?" on page 31 of their magazines. Ask them to identify the differences. Help them know that photos they see of people in magazines are often touched up by photographers using computer programs.
- Ask the girls to share how much they compare themselves to what the world says they should look like. Explain that buying a particular brand of clothing or shoes is one way preteens conform to what the world says they need to look like on the outside.

For Guys Only

- Invite boys to look through the sports pages or magazines.
- Direct them to identify any of the pictures they think might have been touched up prior to printing.
- Guide boys to compare the pictures in "What's the Difference?" on page 31 of their magazines. Ask them to identify the differences. Help them know that photos they see of people in magazines are often touched up by photographers using computer programs.
- Discuss whether the pictures of people in magazines and on TV accurately portray the way people look in real life.
- Pose the following questions for discussion:
  - » What does the world say a guy needs to look like to be attractive to girls? (*big muscles, tall, tough, handsome, and so forth*)
  - » What does the world say a girl needs to look like to be attractive to guys? (*skimpy clothes, immodest clothing, long legs, and so forth*)
- Ask the boys to share how much they compare themselves to what the world says they should look like. Explain that buying a particular brand of clothing or shoes is one way preteens conform to what the world says they need to look like on the outside.

Get Ready: Girls Only
- FLYTE magazine (page 31)
- department store ad pages or a catalog of teenage girls' clothes
- poster board
- scissors
- glue

Get Ready: Guys Only
- FLYTE magazine (page 31)
- sports magazines or sports pages from newspapers

What's the Difference?
There are 21 differences between the two photos. Can you or your preteens find them all? For complete list, check out *www.lifeway.com/flyte*.

UNIT 2 CHANGE

Get Ready - Girls Only
- sticky notes
- poster board
- markers

Get Ready - Guys Only
- table tennis ball

Together: My Answer >>>

For Girls Only
- Guide girls to find and read the following Scriptures:
  - » 1 Samuel 16:7
  - » Proverbs 31:30
  - » 1 Peter 3:3-4
  - » 1 Timothy 2:9-10
  - » Genesis 1:27
- Discuss ways girls can honor God with their looks. (For example, dress modestly, stay healthy, and so forth.)
- Guide girls to write words and phrases from the verses on sticky notes and stick them onto the poster board.
- Encourage each girl to choose one verse to remember when she feels badly about her appearance.

For Guys Only
- Form two teams of boys. Direct teams to stand at opposite sides of a table, facing each other.
- Place a table tennis ball in the center of the table. Explain that teams will blow the ball, trying to get it to fall off the table on the opposite side. Each time the ball is blown off, the winning team will listen to a statement, decide whether they agree or disagree, and explain what God says about each statement.
- Read the following statements as the game is played. Add additional statements as needed:
  - » It's OK to make fun of people's looks as long as they don't hear you.
  - » Wearing the right brand of shoes is important.
  - » Girls only like guys who are tall.
  - » God has a plan for your physical growth.
  - » Boys grow at different rates.
  - » Only good-looking guys are successful.
  - » Hanging out with weird-looking people makes you unpopular.
- Congratulate the winning team. Emphasize that God's Word is the ultimate source of truth. The world's views are constantly changing.

Over and Out
- Dismiss preteens with these final thoughts:
  - » It's normal to care what people think about your looks.
  - » Man looks at outward appearance, but God looks at the heart.
  - » Find your security in who God is, not in the way you look.
- Pray and thank God that His plan includes people of all different shapes, sizes, and colors.

UNIT 3
FAMILY

Memory Passage: Psalm 133:1

Session 1: What Is a Perfect Family?
- Bible passage: Genesis 37:1-11
- There is no perfect family. This week's session will help preteens realize that all families face challenges.

Session 2: Is My Family Broken?
- Bible passage: Genesis 37:12-36
- Every family has struggles. This week preteens will learn that God is always at work in their families' problems.

Session 3: Is There Hope for My Family?
- Bible passage: Genesis 40–45
- Every family has problems. This week preteens will begin to discover strategies to live peacefully with family members and others.

Session 4: How Can My Family Work Together?
- Bible passage: Genesis 50:15-21
- Families are stronger when they work together. This session will help preteens learn that they can get along with their family members.

Bonus Session: Living High or Higher Living?
- Bible passage: Ephesians 5:15-21
- Preteens struggle with the dangers of drugs and alcohol. This week's session will help preteens develop an awareness of the dangers of drugs and alcohol.

Sarah Underhill wrote the Family study. She lives in Hendersonville, Tennessee. She has five children and loves working alongside her husband, a K-5 pastor, with the preteens at their church.

UNIT 3 FLYTE PREP

Other FLYTE Necessities:

FLYTE DVD
The FLYTE DVD has everything you need to enhance media usage with your preteens. Take advantage of the great DVD episodes every week: a countdown clock, Weird of the Day video, teaching video, memory passage music video, and much more.

FLYTE CD-ROM
All the teacher helps, articles, and activity helps you could ever want are found on the CD-ROM. And, because it's important to keep parents in the loop, we've included parent letters for you to e-mail or mail parents (like with a stamp!) to give them a heads-up as to what you will be studying. Take time to explore the entire FLYTE CD-ROM so you don't miss something awesome.

FLYTE Learner Magazine
The FLYTE magazine for preteens is designed to really get your preteens' attention. Exciting graphics, relevant articles, and fun activities will enhance your session as well as provide a resource that preteens can take home and use for future reference. You'll want to buy one for every preteen in your class!

For updates and information, find FLYTE online at
www.lifeway.com/flyte

Session 1: What Is A Perfect Family?
You will need:
- DVD: What Is A Perfect Family? Episodes
- CD-ROM Items 19, 20, 21, 22
- FLYTE magazine (pages 35-37)
- 2 large pieces of paper
- markers

Session 2: Is My Family Broken?
You will need:
- DVD: Is My Family Broken? Episodes
- CD-ROM Items 20, 23, 24, 25, 26
- FLYTE magazine (pages 38-40)
- 3 numbered cubes, set of jacks, small toys and balls
- chart paper, markers
- watch or timer

Session 3: Is There Hope for My Family?
You will need:
- DVD: Is There Hope for My Family? Episodes
- CD-ROM Items 20, 27, 28
- FLYTE magazine (pages 41-43)
- colored pencils
- blindfolds (optional)

Session 4: How Can My Family Work Together?
You will need:
- DVD: How Can My Family Work Together? Episodes
- CD-ROM Item 20, 29
- FLYTE magazine (pages 44-46)
- medium-sized rock for each preteen

Bonus Session: Living High or Higher Living?
You will need:
- FLYTE DVD
- CD-ROM Items 30, 31
- FLYTE magazine (pages 47-49)
- large sheets of paper
- permanent marker
- 3 paper wads
- sticky notes
- griddle, pancake mix
- chocolate chips, whipped topping, sprinkles, fruit, syrup, margarine, and other pancake toppings
- fruit juice, flour tortillas, saltine crackers
- paper plates, disposable cups, eating utensils

WHAT IS A PERFECT FAMILY?

Session Overview

Creating a silly skit, studying the family issues Joseph faced, taking a look at TV families, and studying God's expectations for families will help preteens learn that there is no perfect family.

Teacher Bible Study >>>

The perfect family. Does it exist? Do you look around at other families and think, *Wow, they've really got it together!*? Their kids seem to "get" a spiritual concept more, their traditions seem so special, they always seem to have fun, and they never even disagree! The list could go on and on.

But reality eventually strikes, and you learn the truth about that family—they aren't perfect either. Not every family has the same struggles, but every family has struggles. A Bible study teacher reminded me recently that God chose *my* family for *my* children. He knew our family was the right one to raise these specific children to do the specific tasks He has in store for them. My own parents were chosen specifically to make me who I am today. The only "perfect" family is the one God created just for you.

During this unit, preteens will be looking at Joseph's family. He could have made a long list of his family's faults. Check out Genesis 37:1-11 to see just a few of Joseph's family issues. Yet God used those faults to put Joseph in the exact place He wanted him. This unit will help preteens learn to not focus on the problems but to be watching for how God wants to use them in their families.

Pray. Ask God to help you be sensitive to each preteen's unique family issues. Pray that they will appreciate their families as the ones God chose just for them.

FLYTE Plan

There is no perfect family. This week's session will help preteens realize that all families face challenges.

Bible Study
Genesis 37:1-11

Memory Passage
Psalm 133:1

Level of Biblical Learning
(Family): Families are a part of God's plan for providing for my physical, spiritual, mental, social, and emotional needs.

Get Ready
- "Family Session 1: Takeoff," "The Rocks: Perfect Family (Feature)" (DVD)
- Item 19: "Perfect Family Scenarios" (CD-ROM)
- FLYTE magazine (page 35)

Get Started >>>

Takeoff
- Play "Family Session 1: Takeoff" (DVD) three minutes before the designated start time for the session.
- Allow preteens a minute or two to talk about the Weird of the Day.

The Perfect Family
- Tell preteens that today they will be learning about what makes a perfect family.
- Form teams of four or five preteens.
- Allow each team to draw one card from "Perfect Family Scenarios" (Item 19).
- Instruct each team to create a quick skit depicting how the perfect family would act out the scenario.
- Allow each team to act out its scenario.
- OPTION: If you have more than five groups, allow two groups to act out the same scenario.

Debrief
- Ask preteens the following questions:
  » How realistic were these scenarios?
  » Would you really want to live in a family that was perfect all of the time? Why or why not?
  » How do you think God feels about families' imperfections?

Depends on the Day
- Direct preteens to the "Depends On the Day" (page 35) in the FLYTE magazine.
- Instruct preteens to read the instructions and take a few minutes to think about how their families affect them.
- Allow preteens time to fill in each column by listing the pros and cons of their own families.

The Rocks: Perfect Family
- Cue the DVD and play "The Rocks: Perfect Family."
- Debrief the video by asking the following questions:
  » What did Rocklet think about his own family?
  » What did Rocklet think about the Cells?
  » How did Rocklet's opinion of the Cells change?
- Remind preteens that the Rocks can serve as a reminder that there really is no perfect family.

Faith: God's Answer >>>

Introduction

- Direct preteens to page 35 in the FLYTE magazine.
- Invite a volunteer to read the introduction in the box to the right.
- Allow preteens to name the faults they already know about Joseph's family.
- Explain that most families in the Bible were not even close to perfect. Ask preteens to identify other people in the Bible they know had problems in their families. (For example: Adam and Eve, Cain and Abel, King David, Jacob and Esau, Jesus' brothers.)

Memory Passage: Psalm 133:1

- Call attention to the "Psalm 133:1 Poster" (Item 20) and invite preteens to read it aloud.
- Challenge preteens to memorize the verse during this unit.
- Share the following background information about this verse:
  - » Psalm 133 was written by King David.
  - » It is sometimes referred to as "a song of brotherhood."
  - » The term brothers actually referred to the Israelites; however, the verse can also be applied to families including mom, dad, and siblings.
  - » Ephesians 4:3 states that Christians are to keep a spirit of peace. Family members should live in peace with one another.
- Allow preteens to discuss what they think Psalm 133:1 means.
- Direct preteens to the memory passage section (page 33) in the FLYTE magazine.
- Challenge them to write the passage in their own words.
- OPTION: Cue the DVD to "Harmony" and play the music video.

Study the Bible: Genesis 37:1-11

- Direct preteens to open the FLYTE magazines to "In and Out of Control" on page 35.
- Explain that while they read through the passage today, they should identify problems in Joseph's family. Guide preteens to list problems beyond Joseph's control and things Joseph could control in the corresponding magazine columns.

Joseph's Family

- Direct preteens to open their Bibles to Genesis 37.
- Invite a volunteer to read Genesis 37:1-2 aloud.
- Explain some of Joseph's family history. Touch on each of these points briefly:
  - » Israel had chosen to stay on his family's land. Esau had left, but Israel wanted to live on the land God intended for them.
  - » Joseph's father had many wives as most men did in those days. More wives meant more children, which meant more help with the chores. Joseph's mother, Rachel, was Jacob's

Get Ready
- "Harmony (Music Video)," "Joseph (FLYTE Option)" (DVD)
- Item 20: "Psalm 133:1 Poster" (CD-ROM)
- FLYTE magazine (pages 35, 36)

UNIT 3 FAMILY

favorite wife—the one he truly loved.
- » As shepherds, the sons were responsible for keeping the sheep safe—livestock was a family's version of a savings account.
- » Israel had asked Joseph to let him know how things in the fields were going, but Joseph's brothers were angry he tattled
- Guide preteens to examine the "In and Out of Control" segment titled "Joseph's Family" (page 36) in the FLYTE magazine.
- Allow a few minutes for preteens to record Joseph's family problems and answer the questions in the magazine.

Serious Favoritism
- Invite a volunteer to read Genesis 37:3-4 aloud.
- Direct preteens to the "Serious Favoritism" segment (page 36) in the magazine.
- Allow preteens a few moments to read through the Scripture passage and record the problems in Joseph's family.
- Discuss what preteens wrote in each column and why.
- Give a few moments for preteens to answer the questions in their magazines.
- Discuss what, if anything, Joseph could have done when his father showed him such extreme favoritism.

Bowing Dreams
- Invite a volunteer to read Genesis 37:5-9 aloud.
- Direct preteens to the "Bowing Dreams" segment (page 36) in the magazine.
- Allow them to identify any problems and answer the question.
- Explain the meaning behind the dreams. Touch on these points briefly:
    - » The brothers' sheaves of corn bowing to Joseph's sheaf of corn represented the portion of the passage preteens will study in a few weeks when the brothers ran out of food and had to come to Joseph for help.
    - » In Hebrew, *sun* is a feminine word that represents the mother of the family. *Moon* is a masculine word that represents the father (Israel), and the eleven stars represented the brothers.

Dream Reactions
- Invite a volunteer to read Genesis 37:10-12 aloud.
- Direct preteens to the "Dream Reactions" segment (page 36) in the magazine.
- Allow preteens to identify any problems and answer the question.
- Discuss their answers.
- OPTION: Play the FLYTE Option: "Joseph" (DVD).

Life: World's Answer >>>

Get Ready
- FLYTE magazine (page 37)
- 2 large pieces of paper
- markers

TV Families
- Guide preteens to list the names of television show families on one of the large pieces of paper.
- Allow preteens to share a few characteristics of the families listed.
- Encourage preteens to think about each family and whether the show portrays typical American families in a realistic way.
- Direct preteens to "TV Families" (page 37) in the magazine.
- Allow a few minutes for preteens to read and answer the questions at the top of the page.

Families Around the World
- Attach a large sheet of paper to a focal wall.
- Ask preteens to list all the different types of families they can think of. (For example: grandparents raising grandchildren, homes with both a mom and dad, single parent homes, and so forth.)
- Lead a discussion about each type of family. Invite a volunteer to add to the list the specific challenges each family type might face.
- TIP: Remember that you may hear different family types than you are used to. If necessary, direct preteens to be non-judgmental.

Society's Solutions
- Direct preteens to "Society's Solutions" (page 37) in their FLYTE magazines.
- Invite a volunteer to read the question aloud.
- Give preteens a few minutes to write down their answers.
- Discuss what solutions the world suggests for those stuck in a family they wish they didn't have. Possible answers may include:
  » Blame problems on others instead of taking personal responsibility.
  » Run away to live with someone else.
  » Avoid daily interaction with their family.
  » Decide parents don't deserve their respect.
  » Blame their bad choices on the mistakes of their family.

UNIT 3 FAMILY

Get Ready
- Items 21, 22: "Family Scripture Strips" "God's Expectations" (CD-ROM)—Print multiple copies for larger groups.
- FLYTE magazine (page 35)

Together: My Answer >>>

God's Expectations
- Direct preteens' attention to the "God's Expectations" poster. For larger groups, form several small groups and complete the activit in groups.
- Distribute "Family Scripture Strips" (Item 21).
- Instruct volunteers to look up the Scriptures in their Bibles and read the verses aloud.
- Encourage preteens to listen for the specific expectation God has for families.
- Discuss what each Scripture reference teaches about God's plans for families.
- Direct preteens to write the Scripture reference beside the matching expectation on the poster. (Answers on CD-ROM.)
- OPTION: Challenge preteens to think of other verses during the week that teach about family relationships. Encourage them to bring in as many Scripture references as they can find that teach families how to treat each other. Display today's references in the room, and add other references brought in during the unit.

Depends on the Day Revisited
- Guide preteens to open their FLYTE magazines to "Depends on the Day" (page 35) and take a second look at the list they created during Get Started.
- Ask them if learning that there is no perfect family has helped them accept the things that drive them crazy about their families.
- Explain that they should remember that all families have different quirks that make them unique—not perfect!

Over and Out
- Dismiss preteens with these final thoughts:
  - » Your family is perfect for you because it's the one in which God placed you.
  - » God has big plans for your family.
  - » Enjoy and appreciate your family's strengths instead of focusing on its faults.
- Pray, thanking God that preteens can trust Him through their problems because His plan is perfect. Ask God to help preteens learn from their families.

IS MY FAMILY BROKEN?

Session Overview

Through Scripture, a frustrating game, and thinking how the world and God would want people to respond to difficult scenarios, preteens will learn that God is always at work in their families.

Teacher Bible Study >>>

As the oldest child, I grew up knowing the complications a younger brother could bring. He got into everything, tattled frequently, and got out of chores because he was "too little." It's obvious from the passage in Genesis 37:12-36 that Joseph's brothers were fed up.

Today's preteens face family problems ranging from sibling rivalry to divorce or abuse. As a parent, I now see the younger brother doesn't have it so easy, and I also know the role of being a responsible adult is not always the cakewalk it once seemed.

In today's passage, Joseph was sitting at the bottom of a well listening to his brothers plotting against him. His tough brothers didn't know what they wanted to do to him, but they had to do something. Can you imagine a young boy's heart while listening to that conversation? But God was working even then. You know from later chapters (Gen. 42–47) that this moment was the beginning of how God would feed Joseph's entire family during a severe famine. Of course Joseph didn't have that perspective at the bottom of the well.

Living in a family can be tough. Even the most solid families are made up of imperfect people who sometimes look out for themselves. As an adult, you have had enough experiences to know that struggles are part of being in a family. Preteens look at problems within families and see something that can't be fixed. The goal of this session is to encourage preteens that families are never beyond the reach of God.

Pray. Ask God to help you be sensitive to the problems preteens are facing in their families and to give you opportunities to encourage them.

FLYTE Plan

Every family has struggles. This week preteens will learn that God is always at work in their families' problems.

Bible Study
Genesis 37:12-36

Memory Passage
Psalm 133:1

Level of Biblical Learning
(Family): God loves and cares for families in all kinds of situations.

Get Ready
- "Family Session 2: Takeoff" (DVD)
- Item 23: "'Igloos and Polar Bears' Rules" (CD-ROM)
- FLYTE magazine (page 38)
- 3 numbered cubes, a set of jacks, small toys and balls

Get Started >>>

Takeoff
- Play "Family Session 2: Takeoff" (DVD) three minutes before the designated start time for the session.
- Allow preteens a minute or two to talk about the Weird of the Day.

A Frustrating Scenario
- Gather preteens around a table with three numbered cubes and other random objects.
- Explain they have a problem to solve with the objects through a game called "Igloos and Polar Bears."
- Begin by tossing the objects onto the table. Tell preteens how many igloos and polar bears are showing in the first example according to the secret pattern. (See CD-ROM for detailed instructions.)
- Repeat several times, allowing time after each set of objects for preteens to attempt to solve the pattern. Tell preteens not to share the solution when they think they've figured it out.
- Provide small hints for preteens when they get frustrated, but the object of this game is that they should feel frustrated for a few minutes. Eventually explain the secret of the game.

Debrief
- Direct preteens to "A Frustrating Scenario" (page 38) in the FLYTE magazine.
- Allow preteens a few minutes to read and answer the questions.
- Discuss the frustration of not having the answers and having no way to get them.
- Explain that today's session is about imperfect families who may seem to have no answers.

No Control
- Direct preteens to "No Control" (page 38) in the FLYTE magazine.
- Share with preteens some areas of your own family life that you would like more control over. Share a small area that might be funny, like needing more ice cream, and a bigger area, like a car that runs without breaking down.
- Direct preteens to list in their FLYTE magazines the areas in their families over which they think they have the least control.

Faith: God's Answer >>>

Memory Passage: Psalm 133:1

- Direct preteens to the memory passage section on page 38 in the FLYTE magazine.
- Challenge them to complete the memory passage by filling in the blanks. Show to "Psalm 133:1 Poster" to check their work.
- OPTION: Cue DVD to "Harmony" and play the music video.
- Allow preteens a few minutes to fill out "Harmony Check" in the magazine. Encourage them to really think about the past week and identify situations in which they promoted harmony and others in which they discouraged harmony.
- Explain that today they will be examining a passage that shows how *not* to live in harmony with brothers.

Study the Bible: Genesis 37:12-36

- Remind preteens of the previous week's lesson in which they learned that no family is perfect.
- Guide preteens to open their Bibles to Genesis 37:12-36.

Who Is In Charge?

- Invite a volunteer to read Genesis 37:12-14.
- Ask the class to identify the assignment Israel gave to Joseph.
- Direct preteens to look at Genesis 37:2 and compare it to Genesis 37:12-14. (*Joseph had angered his brothers with the last bad report, and now his father was asking him to go again!*)
- Discuss how Joseph might have felt when asked to bring back a report about his jealous and angry brothers.
- Direct preteens to the map in their learner magazine and point out that Shechem was about 50 miles north of Joseph's home.
- Read Genesis 37:15-17 aloud and share that the brothers were not where their father thought they were. Joseph then had to travel north about 15 more miles to find them.
- Discuss that even though it had been a long journey, and it would be difficult to bring a bad report back to his father, Joseph did the right thing by obeying.

Trouble Ahead

- Invite a volunteer to read Genesis 37:18-22.
- Share with preteens that other passages in the Bible reveal that Joseph's brothers often solved problems with violence, and Joseph knew this as well.
- Direct preteens to "Joseph's Bad Day" (page 39) in FLYTE magazine. Call attention to the "Trouble Ahead" section. Preteens should list things the brothers might have been already angry about.

Get Ready
- "Harmony (Music Video)" (DVD)
- Items 20, 24: "Psalm 133:1 Poster," "Genesis 37:23-35 Strips" (CD-ROM)
- FLYTE magazine (pages 38, 39)

UNIT 3 FAMILY

The Rest of the Story

- Read Genesis 37:23-35 aloud to preteens.
- Form four teams. Give each team a Scripture passage strip. Direct each team to summarize and retell their passage to the class. Work as one large group to retell the story if your group is small.
- Discuss the events of the story following each team's summary. Ask the following questions after each section:
  » Verses 23-25: What does this passage suggest about his brothers if they were able to eat a meal after they attacked Joseph?
  » Verses 26-28: Why did slavery seem like a better solution to the brothers?
  » Verses 29-32: What did the brothers do to hide their sin from their father?
  » Verses 33-35: What did Joseph's father say he would rather do than be comforted? (*Go down to Sheol*, which means "grave or pit.")
- Direct preteens to the FLYTE magazine section titled "The Rest of the Story" (page 39) and read it aloud.
- Allow them to answer the questions.
- Point out that God knows when people know the right thing to do. No matter what situation is going on in a family, Christians are supposed to keep doing what they know is right—whether or not anyone else is.

Sold!

- Invite a volunteer to read Genesis 37:36.
- Ask preteens to answer the questions in the "Sold!" section of their magazines.
- Point out that God used this situation to provide food for Joseph's family during a famine. God was using a seemingly bad situation for good! Announce that preteens will study the end of this passage in the next two weeks.
- Briefly share with preteens a time in your life when God used a bad situation for something good.

Life: World's Answer >>>

ist It! Race

- Tell preteens that while most of America's family problems no longer involve slavery like Joseph's story, Americans have plenty of family problems.
- Form preteens into teams. Tell preteens their goal is to list as many problems that American families face in the allotted time.
- Set a timer for two minutes. Allow teams to use markers to make their lists on chart paper.
- Guide each team to share its answers with the class.

What to Do: The World Says ...

- Use the same teams and give each team one or two of the "Scenario Cards" (Item 25). If you are running short on time, distribute only one card to each team.
- Direct the team to read each scenario card and determine what solution TV characters, the government, or school officials might give for this situation.
- Allow preteens to share their scenarios and world solutions with the class.

Divorce Statistics

- Tell preteens that one way they may feel their family is broken is when a divorce occurs.
- Read the "Divorce Statistics" (Item 26) from the CD-ROM aloud.
- Discuss with preteens the effects of divorce on families while being sensitive to those in your class who may come from a family affected by divorce.
- Emphasize that preteens cannot control whether or not their parents divorce. It is never a child's fault that divorce occurs.
- Assure preteens whose parents are divorced or are facing divorce that they are loved unconditionally.

Worldly Attitudes

- Direct preteens to "Worldly Attitudes" (page 40) in the FLYTE magazine.
- Allow preteens to complete the chart in this section while identifying common attitudes toward families.
- Preteens should describe evidence they see of those attitudes.
- Encourage preteens to share their charts with the class.
- OPTION: Fill in the chart as a class while discussing each aspect.

Get Ready

- Items 25, 26: "Scenario Cards," "Divorce Statistics" (CD-ROM)
- FLYTE magazine (page 40)
- chart paper
- markers
- watch or timer

UNIT 3 FAMILY

Get Ready
- "Backyard Explorers (Feature)" (DVD)
- Item 25: "Scenario Cards" (CD-ROM)
- FLYTE magazine (page 40)

Together: My Answer >>>

Backyard Explorers
- Play "Backyard Explorers" (DVD).
- Ask preteens if they have ever fought with their siblings or cousin
- Help preteens know that families having occasional differences of opinions is normal.
- Remind preteens that even if siblings, cousins, or parents argue, doesn't mean their families aren't normal. All families have issues but with Jesus there is hope.

What to Do: God's Answers
- Direct preteens' attention to the scenario cards used in the previous section.
- Allow preteens to discuss what God's solution for each of these scenarios would be.
- TIP: If preteens give general answers such as, "Go to God with your problems," encourage them to dig deeper and explain what that would actually look like in a family. (For example, pray with your family every day.)

What's My Role?
- Direct preteens to "What's My Role?" (page 40) in the FLYTE magazines.
- Allow preteens a few minutes to think about things they could improve and work on this week and to fill in the blanks.
- Encourage preteens to share one item from the list with the class. Let preteens know you will be praying for them this week about the things they can do to make their families better.
- Point out that some situations require them to seek help from an adult. It's important that preteens know they *must* seek help in situations of abuse (with themselves or a friend), family stress (like a divorce) with which they are not dealing well, alcohol/drug addictions, and any other potentially dangerous situation. Review people with whom they could talk.

Over and Out
- Dismiss preteens with these final thoughts:
  - » Just because a problem seems hopeless and is frustrating doesn't mean God isn't working.
  - » God sometimes uses bad situations to provide for our familie or to teach us!
  - » Look for things you can do to strengthen your family. You should know that some problems are just for adults to solve. Look for help if a problem seems too big.
- Pray, asking God to help preteens learn, seek Him, and trust that He has a plan during difficult family situations.

IS THERE HOPE FOR MY FAMILY?

Session Overview

While playing a teamwork game, studying Joseph's life in Egypt, and thinking about other families who have faced tragedies, preteens will learn that God can always restore a family when its members are open to His working.

Teacher Bible Study >>>

Preteens want answers in knowing how to deal with the problems in their families. When parents split up, fathers put work ahead of their families, or mothers are short-tempered, preteens feel hopeless and they want answers. But what are they supposed to do?

This week's passage is so important because it shows over and over Joseph's response to tough situations. When Joseph was asked to interpret dreams for Egyptians, he put others' needs first. When Joseph was called to a big job to save a country that was not his own, he put others' needs first. And when confronted with the brothers who had betrayed him, Joseph put others' needs first. Joseph didn't have much control over his life, but he repeatedly did the only thing he could—live in harmony with those around him.

This is a common story that many people scan right over. Dive into Genesis 40–45 this week and look at each choice Joseph faced. Try to find a parallel to the choices in your own life. Is there a big job you aren't really excited about that deserves your best? Is there someone you need to forgive? Is there someone you need to help?

Preteens can be selfish. They need guidance in learning how to put others first. This week's lesson is critical for them to dig into instead of skimming it over.

Pray. Ask God to convict you of areas in which you need to make others a priority. Pray that preteens will be able to do the same.

FLYTE Plan

Every family has problems. This week preteens will begin to discover strategies to live peacefully with family members and others.

Bible Study
Genesis 40–45

Memory Passage
Psalm 133:1

Level of Biblical Learning
(Family): Each person in my family has a contribution to make to the family.

Get Ready
- "Family Session 3: Takeoff" (DVD)
- Item 27: "Blindfolded Obstacles" (CD-ROM)
- FLYTE magazine (page 41)
- blindfolds (optional)

Get Started >>>

Takeoff
- Play "Family Session 3: Takeoff" (DVD) three minutes before the designated start time for the session.
- Allow preteens a minute or two to talk about the Weird of the Da

Human Knots
- Arrange preteens into a circular formation (group at least 4 preteens but no more than 10). Larger groups should make seve circles.
- Guide preteens to stand shoulder-to-shoulder with one hand in the middle of the circle. Each preteen should grab someone else hand.
- Lead each preteen to reach into the circle with his or her second hand and grab a second person's hand. Each preteen should hav both arms in the circle with each hand holding a different person hand.
- Challenge preteens to untangle themselves without letting go of the hands they are holding. This may require stepping over, ducking under, twisting, turning, and a lot of giggling!
- OPTION: If this game does not work for your group, try "Blindfolded Obstacles" (Item 27).

Debrief
- Ask preteens the following questions:
  - » What did you have to do in order to succeed at this game? (be patient, work together, depend on others, look out for others)
  - » How does this relate to families succeeding in difficult times?
- Explain that today's lesson will focus on how families can find hor in difficult situations. This requires patience and putting others' needs first—much like the game they just completed.
- Direct preteens to "Hot Points" (page 41) in the FLYTE magazine
- Allow a few minutes for them to rate the situations.
- Encourage preteens to keep their family's lowest-scoring area in mind during the lesson today.

Faith: God's Answer >>>

Memory Passage: Psalm 133:1

- Prior to class, hide the words from "Memory Mix-Up" (Item 28) in various places around the room.
- Tell preteens that they have one minute to find all of the words to their memory passage and put them in order on the floor.
- Allow the class to check their work using the "Psalm 133:1 Poster" (Item 20).
- OPTION: Cue DVD to "Harmony" and play the music video.

Study the Bible: Genesis 40-45

- Ask preteens to open their Bibles to Genesis 40–45. Tell them they will be reading portions of this passage.
- Direct preteens to open their FLYTE magazines to "Hope for Joseph" (page 41).

The Dreamer Interprets

- Invite a volunteer to read Genesis 40:5-8 aloud.
- Encourage preteens to answer the "Hope for Joseph" question in their magazines about the passage.
- Discuss that Joseph had no reason to help the baker or cupbearer. Both were in jail like him, and he had no way of knowing if they could ever help him get out of jail. Joseph's main motivation for interpreting their dreams was their visible distress, and he interpreted their dreams for their own best interest.

An Interpretation Means Freedom

- Explain that when the cupbearer realized Pharaoh needed help interpreting a dream, he remembered that Joseph had interpreted his dream correctly while in jail. Pharaoh, the most important man in all of Egypt, soon called for Joseph's help.
- Invite a volunteer to read Genesis 41:15-16 aloud and guide preteens to fill in the blanks in their magazines.
- Allow preteens to use colored pencils to illustrate in their magazines one of Pharaoh's dreams from Genesis 41:17-27.
- Explain that Joseph was again motivated to use his gift for God's glory. Joseph was jailed and enslaved by Egyptians yet he put the needs of Pharaoh and the Egyptians first.
- Give preteens a brief explanation of Pharaoh's dream based upon Joseph's explanation in Genesis 41:28-36.
  - » Very soon, seven years of plentiful crops would come, but they would be followed by seven years of a severe famine.
  - » God wanted Egypt to put aside some of the food from the seven good years to save up for the seven bad years.

Saving Egypt

- Invite a volunteer to read Genesis 41:46-57 aloud.

Get Ready
- "Harmony (Music Video)," "Family Tips from David and Sissy (Feature)" (DVD)
- Items 20, 28: "Psalm 133:1 Poster," "Memory Mix-Up" (CD-ROM)
- FLYTE magazine (pages 41, 42)
- colored pencils

UNIT 3 FAMILY

- Direct preteens to answer the "Saving Egypt" questions (page 42 in their FLYTE magazines.
- Discuss that once again Joseph was able to live in harmony with those around him by acting in the best interest of Pharaoh and all of Egypt. Most people imprisoned in a foreign land would not work to make that land successful or save it from a famine.

Forgiveness and Provision

- Explain that while Joseph had been helping the Egyptians to have food during the famine, his brothers and father had run out of food. Jacob heard Egypt had storehouses of food and sent his sons to Egypt for help. They arrived and approached Joseph to ask for food, but they did not recognize the brother they had sold into slavery years ago. Joseph stayed undercover for a few days to determine whether or not he could trust his brothers.
- Invite a volunteer to read Genesis 45:1-8 aloud.
- Direct preteens to complete the "Forgiveness and Provision" section (page 42) in their magazines.
- Discuss that Joseph was finally given the chance to get revenge on his brothers, but he didn't say even one word against them or show anything other than forgiveness.
- Encourage preteens to scan through Genesis 45:9-23 and name at least five things that Joseph was able to do for his brothers:
    » Ask them to live in Goshen.
    » Give them food for the next five years of famine.
    » Hug and kiss them.
    » Send wagons to pick up women and children.
    » Get all new belongings in Egypt.
    » Give them new clothes and money.
    » Send his father gifts of donkeys and food.
- Explain that Joseph again acted in the best interest of others.

Family Tips from David and Sissy

- Cue the DVD to "Family Tips from David and Sissy."
- Explain that David Thomas and Sissy Goff are Christian counselors who work with preteens every day. They know all about family struggles.
- Play the DVD.
- Debrief the video by letting preteens list on a large sheet of paper the points David and Sissy made. Gently correct any misconceptions.

Life: World's Answer >>>

Getting Along with Others

- Lead a discussion of things that people do in the world when they don't get along with their family members. Share some of the ways families don't get along and allow for discussion:
  - » Divorce
  - » Fighting
  - » Running Away
  - » Revenge
  - » Deceit
- Direct preteens to "Why Can't We Just Get Along?" (page 42) in the FLYTE magazine.
- Challenge preteens to honestly consider each question.
- Invite volunteers to share, reminding them not to share too much information. Be sensitive to preteens who may have endured very hurtful situations.
- Realize that some preteens in your group may have endured deep hurt by family members. Those preteens may need to talk privately with you or a ministry staff member.

My Talents

- Form small groups of preteens.
- Explain that Joseph had a special talent that could have earned him a lot of money and attention. But Joseph recognized that his talent was from God and that he should use it to glorify Him.
- Encourage each group to identify five talents people use to become successful or famous.
- Challenge preteens to think of talents that are unique.
- Allow teams to take turns acting out their talents using charades.
- Discuss how the world tells people to use their talents for their own glory, fame, and wealth.

Get Ready
- FLYTE magazine (page 42)

UNIT 3 FAMILY

Get Ready
- "The Church Is Family (FLYTE Option)" (DVD)
- FLYTE magazine (page 43)

Together: My Answer >>>

Harmonizing

- Explain that to form harmony, musicians will combine two or more notes to make a beautiful sound. These notes cannot be any two random notes; only certain notes can be played simultaneously to produce a pleasant sound. The same is true for families.
- Direct preteens to "Harmonizing" (page 43) in the FLYTE magazines.
- Lead preteens to read about harmony in families and name six simple things they can do this week to promote harmony in their families.
- Invite volunteers to share their "harmony plans." Be prepared to share a brief example of your own.

Restored

- Ask the following questions:
  - » What was Joseph's family like when he last saw them? (*fighting, hateful, selfish*)
  - » What had to happen before their family was restored? (*Joseph was sold into slavery, his brothers were sorry for their actions, and Joseph forgave them.*)
- Emphasize that there is always hope for families if they will allow God to work. Throughout Joseph's life, he had to put the needs of others ahead of his own, but it eventually enabled him to have the relationship with his family that he had always wanted.
- Play the DVD episode, "The Church Is Family."
- Ask preteens the following questions:
  - » Families can be more than the people who live in houses together. Who are the people in your non-relative family?
  - » What are the characteristics of your church family?

Over and Out

- Gather preteens to pray, asking God to help preteens live peacefully with their family members. Dismiss preteens with these final thoughts:
  - » Life is full of tough situations, but you have a choice in how you respond.
  - » Putting others first is sometimes the only (and best!) thing you can do.
  - » God can restore *any* bad situation in your family if you are willing to let Him work.

HOW CAN MY FAMILY WORK TOGETHER?

Session Overview

Preteens will learn about the importance of forgiveness through an object lesson, digging into how Joseph and his brothers handled conflict, and creating a newscast on a modern-day Joseph story.

Teacher Bible Study >>>

Family relationships can be complicated! In fact, many people will admit to dreading the holidays because of the inevitable conflicts. It's not that family members don't love each other or care for one another, but when a conflict arises, it is often shoved under the proverbial rug in order to keep the illusion of a happy family gathering. Problems occur when those family conflicts are never resolved and instead build up over time until there's an emotional explosion.

Resolving conflict in families is hard. Family members have to be aware of private issues the other person is having, personalities that clash, and temperaments of the family member with whom they are at odds. Not to mention that different communication styles and the history of conflict must be considered as well!

This week's passage is a wonderful biblical example of how Christians should resolve conflict. Joseph has many reasons to hold a grudge against his brothers, but he chose again and again to forgive, forget, and move forward in the relationship, giving even more than required. Read through Genesis 50:15-21 several times this week, thinking about Joseph's choice to forgive.

Preteens may just now be realizing some of the conflict that goes on within their extended or nuclear families. Small children are sometimes oblivious, but preteens' ears pick up on everything! The older they get, the harder it can be to forgive. Preteens must learn at a young age that one important key to a healthy family is forgiveness.

Pray. Name your preteens aloud to God, asking Him to soften their hearts toward family members with whom they are in conflict.

FLYTE Plan

Families are stronger when they work together. This session will help preteens learn that they can get along with their family members.

Bible Study
Genesis 50:15-21

Memory Passage
Psalm 133:1

Level of Biblical Learning
(Family): God wants me to show love, respect, cooperation, and consideration for all persons in my family.

Get Ready
- "Family Session 4: Takeoff" (DVD)
- Item 29: "Conflict Quiz" (CD-ROM)
- FLYTE magazine (page 44)
- medium-sized rock for each preteen

Get Started >>>

Takeoff
- Play "Family Session 4: Takeoff" (DVD) three minutes before the designated start time for the session.
- Allow preteens a minute or two to talk about the Weird of the Da

Rock It
- Give each preteen a fist-sized rock as he arrives. Tell him to hold it in one of his hands during the entire lesson but offer no further explanation.
- OPTION: If you cannot find enough large rocks, you could use several smaller rocks or other similarly sized and weighted object like a baseball, bottled water, or small weights.

Copycat
- Direct preteens to stand in a circle.
- Invite one volunteer to be the "guesser" and to leave the room momentarily. When the guesser leaves, the other preteens choos a "leader" to direct movements for the group. The leader should begin the first movement. (Movements might be clapping, jumping, snapping, stomping, singing, dancing, and so forth.)
- Invite the guesser into the room once the group begins. The guesser will stand in the middle of the circle and try to figure out the leader's identity. The leader should wait until the guesser is n looking and change the movement. When the leader changes the movement, all of the others in the circle must quickly change thei movements to copy the leader. The round ends when the guesse identifies the leader.

Debrief
- Ask students what the circle members did to make the game mos challenging for the guesser.
- Tell preteens that today they will be identifying how to work together with their families, even during conflict.
- Pass out the "Conflict Quiz" (Item 29) from the CD-ROM and encourage preteens to complete it honestly.
- Direct preteens to "Conflict Quiz" (page 44) in their magazines.
- Encourage preteens to think about how they handle conflict as they answer the questions about the quiz.

Faith: God's Answer >>>

Memory Passage: Psalm 133:1

- Display the memory verse poster, and invite preteens to read it aloud. Then put the poster away.
- Direct preteens to stand in a circle. Choose one person to begin.
- The first person will say the first word of the memory verse, the second person should say the second word, and so on.
- If a person says the wrong word or responds too slowly, she should step out of the circle.
- Preteens should continue repeating the verse, getting faster each time, until only one person remains.
- Repeat as time and interest allows.
- Encourage volunteers to share if they have changed anything about a family relationship this month as a result of this verse.
- OPTION: Cue the DVD to "Harmony" and play the music video.

Study the Bible: Genesis 50:15-21

- Ask preteens to open their Bibles to Genesis 50:15.
- Direct preteens to turn to page 44 in FLYTE magazine.

First Steps

- Invite a volunteer to read Genesis 50:15-17 aloud.
- Direct preteens to "Pursuing Peace" in their magazines and answer the "First Steps" questions.
- Ask preteens why Joseph's brothers sent a message instead of going to speak with Joseph directly. Explain the situation:
  » Joseph's brothers knew he loved their father deeply. They were afraid now that their father was gone, Joseph would not feel obligated to treat them with kindness.
  » They now realized what they had done to Joseph and how wrong it was, and they weren't exactly sure that Joseph could forgive them without any repercussions.
  » They wanted to know where Joseph stood, but they thought going before him directly might be too risky. They sent a message first, telling him of their father's request.

True Repentance

- Invite a volunteer to read Genesis 50:18 aloud.
- Direct preteens to answer the "True Repentance" questions on page 44 of the magazine.
- Discuss the courage it must have taken for Joseph's brothers to bow before him knowing he was one of the most powerful men in Egypt. They were thankful for the grace Joseph offered them when he had given them food and cared for their families. But they were willing to face whatever punishment Joseph wanted to give them.
- Compare the remorse of Joseph's brothers with that of Peter's after he denied Christ three times. (See Luke 22:54-62.) Peter did

Get Ready
- "Harmony (Music Video)" (DVD)
- Item 20: "Psalm 133:1 Poster" (CD-ROM)
- FLYTE magazine (pages 44, 45)

UNIT 3 FAMILY

not try to explain himself to Jesus, to defend himself, or get angr
and walk away. Peter simply knew he was wrong, and he showed
true remorse over his sin by weeping.

Joseph's Response
- Invite a volunteer to read Genesis 50:19-22 aloud.
- Direct preteens to answer the "Joseph's Response" questions on
  page 45 of their magazines.
- Discuss that Joseph acknowledged his brothers' plan for evil.
  Forgiving does not mean ignoring what happened. Joseph
  chose to not discuss it or bring it up detail by detail; he knew his
  brothers were sorry, and there was no reason to go through every
  mistake they had made.
- Point out that Joseph acknowledged that God had allowed this
  because He had a plan. Refer back to the previous sessions in thi
  unit that have been building toward this moment. For example,
  Joseph in the bottom of a well, with no hope—this was the
  moment for which God had been planning.
- Encourage preteens to look up the other three verses listed in the
  magazine (Matthew 6:14-15; Matthew 5:23-24; and Luke 11:3-4)
  and write what each says about forgiveness.

Prayer of Forgiveness
- Lead each preteen to think of a family member with whom she is
  in conflict.
- Guide preteens to pray a silent prayer asking God to end the
  conflict.
- Close by praying for preteens to choose to live in peace with thei
  family members.

Life: World's Answer >>>

Mary's Problem PSA
- Cue the DVD to "Mary's Problem PSA."
- Explain that a public service announcement (or PSA) can be used to help the public learn about different topics of interest.
- Explain that watching an old PSA is funny today, especially when filmmakers do a little modernizing. Play the video.
- Debrief the PSA by allowing preteens to share what they found most funny.

Joseph's Story Today PSAs
- Form groups of three to five preteens.
- Encourage groups to think about how Joseph's story would go if it happened today. Imagine hearing on the news that a group of brothers sold their youngest brother into slavery to another nearby country. Joseph should react the way society would expect him to act; his choices would be based upon making himself happy and more famous.
- Tell groups to develop a likely PSA that would relay this story in modern-day terms. Make sure preteens address the following questions:
  » Of what modern-day things might his brothers have been jealous?
  » What family conflicts are most common in today's society that Joseph and his family might have faced?
  » How would a man who had become an important government official in another country treat brothers who had now come to beg for food?
- Allow five minutes for each group to prepare its PSA, then allow each group to present its newscast to the class.
- Discuss after each presentation whether it was an accurate presentation of what would happen in today's society.

What Good Are Siblings?
- Direct preteens to "What Good Are Siblings?" (page 45) in the FLYTE magazine.
- Encourage preteens to fill in the blanks while thinking about the pros and cons of siblings. If a preteen does not have a sibling, he or she could list the pros and cons of having cousins or list the pros and cons of a friend's siblings.
- Discuss these responses as a class.
- Remind preteens not to slander their brothers and sisters in their sharing time.

Get Ready
- "Mary's Problem PSA (Feature)" (DVD)
- FLYTE magazine (page 45)

Get Ready
- "Family Serves Together (FLYTE Option)" (DVD)
- FLYTE magazine (page 46)

Together: My Answer >>>

Me? Drive Someone Crazy?
- Direct preteens to "Me? Drive Someone Crazy?" on page 46 of their learner magazines.
- Encourage each preteen to fill in the chart honestly, noting his strengths and weaknesses in his family.

Families Working Together
- Show preteens the video "Family Serves Together" (DVD).
- Encourage preteens to think of ways their families could serve together.

Rock It
- Ask preteens their thoughts about having to hold the rocks today and how it made their tasks harder.
- Explain that the rock represents something they refuse to forgive. When you choose to not forgive someone, it affects your daily life, whether you realize it or not. Imagine if there were multiple rocks! God tells you to forgive because it's best for you and your relationships.
- Remind preteens of Ephesians 4:26: "Don't let the sun go down on your anger."

Over and Out
- Dismiss preteens with these final thoughts:
  » God created your family members in a special way so that you can learn from each other.
  » Conflict is hard to resolve, but it is one of the most important keys to living in harmony with your family.
  » Ask for forgiveness in a way that shows you are truly sorry, and forgive easily.
- Pray and ask God to help preteens show love, respect, cooperation, and consideration for all persons in their families.

BONUS: LIVING HIGH OR HIGHER LIVING?

ession Overview

reteens are often faced with decisions concerning drugs or alcohol.
this session, preteens will develop an awareness of peer pressure
nd the dangers of substance abuse. They will be challenged to live
rug free instead of living high, understanding that as believers in
hrist, they are called to higher living.

Teacher Bible Study >>>

"Come on, it's just one drink! What's the harm in that?" "I can quit
nytime I want!" "It's my body, and I'll put into it what I want."
Chances are you have heard one of these statements or something
milar. You don't have to look far to discover just how prevalent drugs
nd alcohol are in the world today and how misinformed people are
bout them. Using alcohol and drugs is not just something that your
reteens face. As an adult, you face the same choices as to what
nd of a high you are going to live on. You can choose to live high
r understand that, as a believer in Jesus, you have been called to a
igher living than the rest of the world.

While the Bible does not specifically identify every drug or choice of
ariety of alcohol, it does have some principles to consider. Since your
ody is not your own, and you have been bought through the blood
f Jesus, adopt His set of standards for your life.

In Ephesians 5:15-21, Paul challenges believers to be careful of how
hey live their lives before others. He tells them to not be drunk with
ine because when they do, they do not have control of their bodies,
nd their actions are no longer godly or Spirit filled.

Before making preteens aware of the dangers of drugs and alcohol,
ok closely at these issues yourself. Are you excusing the usage of
rugs and alcohol because the world says they are OK? Listen to
aul's words: "Don't be foolish, but understand what the Lord's will is."

ray. Ask God to give you a deeper understanding of the dangers of
rugs and alcohol and the conflict that it has with His will for your life.
ray that He will give you the ability to accept the call to higher living.

FLYTE Plan

*Preteens struggle with the
dangers of drugs and alcohol.
This week's session will help
preteens develop an awareness
of the dangers of drugs and
alcohol.*

Bible Study
Ephesians 5:15-21

Level of Biblical Learning
(Self): Self-control and
obedience to God can help me
stand up to peer pressure. My
self-control honors God and
benefits me.

Get Ready
* large sheets of paper, markers
* 3 paper wads—Write the words *thought*, *feeling*, and *advice* on separate wads.
* permanent marker
* OPTION: FLYTE magazine (page 47)

Get Started >>>

A Note About FLYTE Bonus Sessions
* Bonus sessions are shorter than normal sessions. If the issue discussed is relevant to your preteens, please use it.
* If the issue is too mature for your preteens, use the fellowship ide on page 89.

Positive I.D.
* Prior to students arriving, hang two large sheets of paper on opposite walls. Write *Good* on one sheet, and write *Bad* on the other.
* Direct preteens to write on the papers either good things that drugs do (for example, prescription drugs help heal) or bad thing that drugs do (for example, cause loss of body control). OPTION: Allow preteens to create their "Positive I.D." lists on page 47 of their FLYTE magazines.
* Read both of the lists aloud. Tell preteens that today that they wil develop a greater awareness of drugs and alcohol.

Share Circle
* Instruct preteens to stand in a circle around the room. Provide three prepared paper wads. Tell preteens to toss the paper wads to each other until you tell them to stop.
* Signal preteens to stop. Depending on which paper wad a preteen is holding, he should share his thoughts, feelings, or advice that he would share with someone who is considering using drugs or alcohol.
* Continue until the majority of the group has had the opportunity to answer.
* Explain that a drug is something that effects your body in one wa or another. When preteens think of drugs, they might often think of pills a person takes, but drugs also include alcohol, caffeine, nicotine, and other substances.

Faith: God's Answer >>>

Get Ready
- FLYTE magazine (page 48)
- large sheet of paper

Study the Bible: Ephesians 5:15-21
- Tell preteens to open their Bibles to Ephesians 5:15-21.
- Share some background information about the Book of Ephesians:
  » Ephesians was written by Paul.
  » Paul wrote the letter while in prison, though no one is sure whether he was in prison in Rome or in Caesarea.
  » The letter was written to the church at Ephesus.

Walking Like the Wise
- Allow volunteers to explain what the word *wise* means.
- Tell preteens to read the definition of *wise* on page 48 in their magazines.
- Ask a volunteer to read Ephesians 5:15-16 in her Bible.
- Encourage preteens to explain what "walking like the wise" might mean. Guide preteens to write their thoughts on page 48 of their magazines.

Don't Be Foolish
- Direct preteens to "Don't Be Foolish" (page 48) in the FLYTE magazine. Choose a volunteer to read Ephesians 5:17-18 aloud.
- Call for preteens to share what it means to be drunk with wine and write it on the large sheet of paper.
- Ask: "What other things can inhibit people's bodies?"
- List their answers on the large sheet of paper. (Possible answers include sniffing glue, smoking pot, and so forth.)
- Tell preteens that when Ephesians was written, the use of drugs was not an issue like it is today. If it was, Paul might have written to stay away from drugs as well.
- Paul said that using alcohol recklessly was foolish.

Wise Living
- Lead preteens to read Ephesians 5:19-21 and complete the "Wise Living" section (page 48) in the FLYTE magazine.
- Tell preteens that this type of activity honors God and tells the world that Jesus is Lord of your life.
- Guide preteens to form groups and rewrite this section of Scripture in their magazines using their own words.
- Allow groups to share their responses.

Pray
- Ask God to help preteens stand up against the pressures of the world.
- Ask Him to give preteens courage to talk to their parents or a trusted adult if they are being pressured to try drugs or alcohol.

Get Ready
- Item 30: "Statistically Speaking" (CD-ROM)
- FLYTE magazine (page 49)

Get Ready
- Item 31: "Choose Drug Free" (CD-ROM)—Print one for each preteen.

Life: World's Answer >>>

Statistically Speaking
- Gather a group of 10 preteens (or 5 if your group is small). Ask th group to stand at the front of the room.
- Tell the group that you will share from the FLYTE magazine statistics of drug and alcohol use among American students.
- Follow the "Statistically Speaking" directions on the CD-ROM. Pause for discussion and reactions to the statistics you read from "Statistically Speaking" (page 49).
- Ask preteens to share whether or not they were surprised by the statistics. Why or why not?

Together: My Answer >>>

Choose To Live Drug Free
- Ask preteens what they have learned about how God feels about drugs and alcohol today.
- Challenge them to live drug and alcohol free.
- Distribute the "Choose Drug Free" CD-ROM item to each preteen.
- Ask a volunteer to read the challenge aloud.
- Tell preteens if they accept the challenge, they should sign the cards and keep them in a place where they can be reminded to honor God with their bodies and stay away from drugs and alcohol.

Over and Out
- Remind preteens of these final thoughts:
  » The Bible says your body is God's temple. Honor it by not putting harmful substances in it.
  » You will be pressured to try drugs and alcohol by your friends Think about how you will react when a friend offers you drugs
  » Remember that there are other harmful substances like sniffin glue, taking someone else's prescription medicine, and so forth that are harmful to the body and should be avoided.
- Pray, asking God to protect preteens from the dangers of drugs and alcohol. Pray that each preteen will commit to keeping his body pure of harmful substances.

FLAT FOOD FUN

Flat Food Relay
- Form two teams. Tell teams to stand in a single file line.
- Give a flour tortilla to the person at the front of each line.
- Tell preteens to pass the tortilla over-under style to the end of the line. When the tortilla reaches the end of the line, the preteen at the end should run to the front of the line and repeat the process. Continue until each preteen has returned to his original position in line.
- Congratulate the team that finishes first.

Tortilla Toss
- Tell preteens they will now see who can toss their tortillas the furthest.
- Give one preteen a tortilla and ask her to toss it like a frisbee. Give her a sticky note to mark the spot where the tortilla lands, and give the tortilla to the next player to avoid wasting a new tortilla.
- Continue in the same manner until each preteen has had an opportunity to toss the tortilla.
- Congratulate the preteen with the best toss.

Cracker Quotes
- Give preteens a few minutes to write a silly sentence using only words with the letter *F* in them. Sentences should also include the word *FLYTE*.
- Hand each preteen a cracker. Tell preteens they will take turns reading their silly sentences, but the only catch is that they have to hold the crackers in their mouths. They may break the crackers into smaller pieces.
- Encourage preteens to listen carefully to see who can speak the clearest. Congratulate the preteen who states his sentence most clearly.

Party with Pancakes
- Fix pancakes according to the directions on the box.
- Distribute cups, eating utensils, and paper plates. Allow preteens to add their favorite toppings to the pancakes.
- Give preteens juice to drink.
- Pray and bless the meal, thanking God that preteens know more about heaven, God's plan for change, and family relationships.
- Remind preteens of the topics discussed in FLYTE Volume 1 and ask preteens if they have any additional thoughts or comments about the different topics.
- Cue DVD to the preteens' favorite videos from Volume 1 and let them watch while they eat.

Get Ready
- FLYTE DVD
- pancake mix—Gather ingredients indicated on box.
- griddle
- chocolate chips, whipped topping, sprinkles, fruit, syrup, margarine, and other pancake toppings
- fruit juice
- flour tortillas
- saltine crackers
- sticky notes
- paper plates, disposable cups, eating utensils

BONUS

COMING IN VOLUME 2

Unit 1: God's Plan
Memory Passage: John 6:39-40
Session 1: What Is God's Plan for the World?
  Bible passage: Psalm 96:1-13
Session 2: What Is God's Plan for Me?
  Bible Passage: Esther 1:15-20; 3:1-14; 4:13-17; 5:1-5; 8:1-8
Session 3: How Can I Live Out God's Plan for Me?
  Bible Passage: 1 Samuel 3
Session 4: How Can I Help Others Discover God's Plan?
  Bible Passage: John 1:35-42

Unit 2: Emotions
Memory Passage: Philippians 4:6-7
Session 1: How Can I Control Anger?
  Bible passage: 1 Samuel 25
Session 2: How Can I Deal with Fear?
  Bible passage: Matthew 6:25-34
Session 3: How Can I Handle Depression?
  Bible passage: Job 1
Session 4: How Can I Cope with Grief?
  1 Samuel 20:18-25,35-42; 2 Samuel 1

Unit 3: Respect
Memory Passage: Philippians 2:3-4
Session 1: What Is Respect and Why Should I Give It?
  Bible Passage: Philippians 2:3-11
Session 2: Do They Deserve My Respect?
  Bible Passage: 1 Peter 2:11-17; Acts 10:9-34; 11:1-17
Session 3: Why Respect Those Who Are Different?
  Bible Passage: Luke 10:25-37
Session 4: How Can I Earn Respect?
  Bible Passage: Luke 2:1-20

Bonus Session: What Does His Birth Mean to Me?
Bible passage: Luke 2:1-20